China's Assertive Posturing in the Indo-Pacific & Prospects for Indo-ASEAN Collaboration

China's Assertive Posturing in the Indo-Pacific & Prospects for Indo-ASEAN Collaboration

EDITED BY
SRUTHI SADHASIVAM

KW Publishers Pvt Ltd
New Delhi

CHENNAI CENTRE FOR CHINA STUDIES

Centre for East Asian Studies
CHRIST UNIVERSITY

www.c3sindia.org

The Chennai Centre for China Studies (C3S), registered under the Tamil Nadu Societies Registration Act 1975 (83/2008 dated 4th April 2008), is a non-profit public policy think tank with the following objectives.

- Carry out in-depth studies of developments relating to China with priority to issues of interest to India such as
    1. Geopolitical, economic and strategic dynamics of India-China relations.
    2. China's internal dynamics.
    3. The Sino-Indian border issue.
    4. China's relations with South Asian countries.
    5. Prospects of Sino-Indian economic and trade relations.
    6. Future evolution of China's politics and its impact on India and the world.
    7. China-India-ASEAN relations.
    8. China's emerging role in SAARC.
    9. Growing importance of South India for Chinese interaction and economic investment.
    10. India-China-Southeast Asia cultural links.
- Suggest viable solutions/policy alternatives on the basis of studies to the strategic planners and decision makers in India on issues of bilateral, regional and global importance.
- Create public opinion, particularly in South India, on the implications arising out of China's emergence as a leading global power.
- Provide a forum for dialogue with China scholars in India and abroad and give space for expression of alternate opinions on China-related topics.
- Provide a sound data base for research on China with special attention to tapping information available in Chinese language material, so as to benefit scholars, media and think tanks in India as well as rest of the world.
- Address the requirements of the business community in India, particularly informing them about the nature of emerging business opportunities and problems while dealing with China.
- Liaise with think tanks specialising on China, both in India and abroad, with the objective of exchanging views.
- Organise lecture discussions and seminars on topics of current interest.
- Interact with institutions of higher learning in South India to create awareness about developments in China.
- Bring out publications relating to China—books, edited volumes, monographs and occasional papers.

ISBN 978-81-980963-0-2 Paperback

Published in India by Kalpana Shukla

KW Publishers Pvt Ltd
4676/21, First Floor, Ansari Road, Daryaganj, New Delhi 110002
Phone: +91-11-43528107
Email: kw@kwpub.in • www.kwpub.in

Printed and bound in India.

Contents

Foreword vii

Prologue ix

Editor's Note xi

Tables, Figures and Maps xv

Acknowledgements xvii

Abbreviations and Acronyms xix

China's Geo-Economic Inroads in Southeast Asia

1. East Asia & China's (Geo-economic) Footprint in Southeast Asia: ASEAN Centrality? 3
Dharish David and Abhisek Kumar Pandey

China's Maritime Influence in the ASEAN Region & Prospects for India-ASEAN Relations

2. Chinese Maritime Strategy and its Impact on Southeast Asia & Beyond: A Philippine Perspective 35
RAdm Rommel Jude G Ong AFP (Retd)

3. China's Maritime Militia in the South China Sea: Implications to ASEAN Countries' Food and Territorial Security 49
Nguyen Hoang Anh Thu

4. The US FONOP Exercises & China's Submarine Patrols in the South China Sea Region: Challenges to ASEAN States' EEZ Rights 62
Jeslyn Tan

5. Viet Nam—India Defence and Security Cooperation: Any New Impetus to Bolster? 77
Nguyen Thi Lan Huong

About the Contributors 88

About the Book 94

Foreword

The very first joint effort of Chennai Centre for China Studies and the Christ University Bangalore in December 2023 facilitated the process of bringing a prestigious university, academia and one of the foremost think tanks specialising in China Studies together that resulted in bringing out this post-event publication that deals with "*China's Assertive Posturing in the Indo-Pacific: Prospects for Indo-ASEAN Collaboration.*"

The event was very well received and had participants from the region to bring in first-hand assessments of China's subtle and not-so-subtle initiatives in the region of great importance to global affairs. It is acknowledged that Indo-Pacific is the new arena of conflict and ASEAN as an entity is central to the emerging nature of power play. The maritime dimensions appear to take centre stage with the happenings in the South China Sea where China seems to be needling most of its maritime neighbours by illegal declaration of most parts of SCS as its own. The economic interdependence in the region with China leading the fray has been the leverage that China applies against its smaller neighbours who are dependent on China's investments for their own growth. The examples of the Belt and Road Initiative that have led countries into a debt trap and the RCEP which provide enough economic handles to China are reasons for the countries in the region to be cautious of China's long-term strategy. ASEAN as a block has not entirely been successful in presenting a common front against Chinese wolf war diplomacy. Even the Code of Conduct is yet to see the light of the day as China prefers to deal with the smaller neighbours from a position of strength.

The emerging nature of power play in the region has witnessed the introduction of QUAD which though not being a military alliance has provided many options for the partnering countries for initiatives to counter China's hegemony. Since the revitalisation of the QUAD, there has been a great interest amongst both developing and developed countries in shaping their Indo-Pacific strategy. ASEAN is no exception and has also been able to articulate its own position on the Indo-Pacific by the ASEAN Outlook on the Indo-Pacific. It is also notable that some of the countries such as Singapore, and South Korea in the region are seriously examining the implications of a possible QUAD plus mechanism. The recent nomenclature of SQUAD includes the Philippines along with USA, Australia and Japan highlighting the seriousness and importance that the Philippines' leadership attaches to China-specific initiatives.

The December conference in Bengaluru highlighted these issues and more with excellent paper presentations by acknowledged resource persons from the countries in the region and also scholars from India. The increasing pressure faced by the Philippines in the maritime domain is indicative of the pattern of coercion by China by use of grey zone warfare that has witnessed the use of military militia and use of disproportionate force to prevent the Philippines from exercising its jurisdiction in its areas despite the verdict of the Permanent Court of Arbitration in 2016.

Issues of convergence and challenges as India and ASEAN members seek to find ways to work together in the face of stiff challenges by China were discussed in detail.

Special thanks also to all the resource persons who ensured that the timelines for submission of the papers were met and the highest quality was maintained in the papers presented. I also take this opportunity to thank our co-hosts led by Professor Manoharan for all the coordination and help in conducting this event which will now be an annual event in Bengaluru.

Sruthi Sadhasivam who was totally in charge of the entire programme from conceptualisation to fruition needs to be complemented and commended for her efforts to obtain all papers and edit them in a time-bound manner to bring out this publication that would be of immense value to students and scholars alike.

Commodore **R. S. Vasan** IN (Retd)

Prologue

China's Assertive Posturing in the Indo-Pacific: Prospects for Indo-ASEAN Collaboration edited by Ms Sruthi Sadhasivam is an outcome of a collaborative International Conference between the Chennai Centre for China Studies (C3S) and Centre for East Asian Studies (CEAS), Christ University, Bangalore. Comprising five chapters, the book looks at two broad dimensions of cooperation between India and ASEAN viz., economic and maritime. This is seen from the perspective of China's assertive posturing in the Indo-Pacific region, both in economic and military domains. In the name of the Belt and Road Initiative (BRI), China has been attempting to establish its security and economic footprints in the region. Beijing's 'Blue Dragon' Strategy, more precisely, is aimed at getting a good strategic grip on the countries of the Indo-Pacific.

As a result, the Indo-Pacific region has of late become more complex and contested. Two principal actors involved in this so-called 'Great Game,' or rather in 'strategic rivalry,' are the United States and China. The other major movers and shakers in the Indo-Pacific region include India, ASEAN, Japan, South Korea, and Australia. While the leanings of Japan, South Korea and Australia are known, India and ASEAN wish to maintain 'strategic autonomy.' Sitting at the centre of the vastly spread Indo-Pacific region, ASEAN is an important component of India's Indo-Pacific strategy, especially when it comes to dealing with China.

There are significant convergences and cooperative elements between the ASEAN Outlook on Indo-Pacific (AOIP) and India's Indo-Pacific

Oceans Initiative (IPOI). There are four broad areas of convergences to note: common values; maintaining balance, neutrality and autonomy in the Indo-Pacific; broad and pluralistic engagements; and issue-based cooperation. In this regard, it is important to highlight seven pillars of India's IPOI: maritime security; maritime ecology; maritime resources; capacity building and resource sharing; disaster risk reduction and management; science, technology and academic cooperation; trade connectivity and maritime transport. These seven pillars are actually in a position to strengthen and broaden base cooperation between India and ASEAN. They are forward-looking and non-sensitive and go with ASEAN's wish to maintain neutrality in the power rivalry in the region.

At the same time, there are challenges as well that range from a lack of cohesion among ASEAN members on the exact role of the organisation in the Indo-Pacific region and the paucity of resources to meet its centrality role in the region. Leveraging the convergences and managing the existing challenges will undoubtedly elevate India-ASEAN relations to a new level. To bolster this cooperation further, India and ASEAN could rope in other entities in the Indo-Pacific region like the Indian Ocean Rim Association (IORA), Indian Ocean Naval Symposium (IONS), Bay of Bengal Initiative for Multi-Sectoral Technical and Economic Cooperation (BIMSTEC) and the like.

Dr N. Manoharan

Editor's Note

The idea behind producing a book was visualised as a conference outcome with the Chennai Centre for China Studies (C3S) hosting a one-day International Conference on ASEAN Centrality in the Indo-Pacific: Prospects and Challenges for Security, Peace & Prosperity in collaboration with the Centre for East Asian Studies (CEAS), Christ (deemed to be) University, Bangalore on the 18th of December, 2023 (Monday) in the premises of Christ (deemed to be) University, Bangalore. The conference sought to understand the Southeast Asian outlook on China's pursuits in the Indo-Pacific Region (IOR). It is in this light, that scholars from the Philippines, Singapore, Vietnam and Malaysia as well as experts on Indonesia and China were invited to share their expertise on this theme. The ultimate goal was to compile a book that presents a comprehensive overview of Southeast Asian policies, responses, and strategies to China's perceived aggressive actions in the IOR with a special emphasis on India's potential contributions to the region's security dynamics.

As the theme of the conference suggests, the book explores the areas of convergence, collaboration and challenges between India and Southeast Asian states; Southeast Asian states' perception of China's endeavours in the Indo-Pacific and their strategies and responses to deal with China. The book is divided into two sections covering the Southeast Asian maritime and economic dimensions along with the India-ASEAN relations in the evolving security landscape of the Indo-Pacific region.

The economic dimension delves into the shifts and evolutions of ASEAN trade vis-a-vis China and East Asia in the changing geopolitical scenario. With ASEAN becoming an increasingly attractive destination for international investment, the book brings out the complexity of the trade dynamics within ASEAN in the face of RCEP, substantial reliance of ASEAN countries on China for their import needs coupled with the US-China tensions in the Indo-Pacific. Key to this study is the application of data-driven analysis to uncover the latest developments and patterns in ASEAN trade.

In the maritime dimension, the book explores the food security of ASEAN states in the face of China's maritime militia and delves into the Philippines' maritime strategy against China. It's been 76 years since the South China Sea dispute started and there seems to be no end to it. In fact, the conflict has been escalating with countries reclaiming lands and militarising the region. We have come to that stage of unconventional warfare where Southeast Asian nations' responses have transitioned from mere verbal sparring to concrete demonstrations of strength and determination in their assertion of interests.

In addition, with the increasing presence of global powers such as the US, China and with the entry of India, the tensions have become more manifest. Both US and China conduct frequent maritime patrols across various parts of the Indian Ocean and that poses a major threat to the sovereignty of the coastal states. In this light, the book examines the role of big powers' submarine patrols in violating ASEAN states' sovereignty from the perspective of law. Further, it explores the possibility of an arms race in the South China Sea with major powers using nuclear submarines on the pretext of exercising their freedom of navigation.

In addition to the US and China, India has risen to prominence, recently it expressed support to the Philippines in upholding peace and security in the Indo-Pacific. Among India's relationships with ASEAN nations, its relations with Vietnam and the Philippines are particularly noteworthy, serving as prime illustrations of the broader India-ASEAN dynamics. The book seeks to address the knowledge gap surrounding India's influence on ASEAN's security landscape. It delves into India's relations with the Philippines and

Vietnam in the defence sector including bilateral defence dialogues and defence exports. Efforts aim at enhancing maritime security cooperation between India and the two Southeast Asian counterparts in the wake of China's assertive moves in the South China Sea.

By and large, the book is a must-read for China enthusiasts interested in decoding China from a Southeast Asian vista.

Sruthi Sadhasivam
Research Officer,
Chennai Centre for China Studies (C3S) &
Coordinator of the C3S-CEAS ASEAN Conference

Tables, Figures and Maps

Tables

1.1	Cumulative FDI into ASEAN member states 2012-2021	8
1.2	Top importer/exporter of ASEAN member states	14
1.3	ASEAN export-import by World, ASEAN, China, USA (2020-2022)	15
1.4	Comparison of historic and projection trends for USA, China, ASEAN and India	28
4.1	PLAN Submarines Active in 2023	67

Figures

1.1	FDI in ASEAN by source countries	7
1.2	Top 5 Export Destinations (% share in value in export for ASEAN Member States (2018-2022)	10
1.3	Top 5 Import Destinations and % share in value in import for ASEAN Member States (2018-2022)	12
1.4	Arrangements in Indo-Pacific	17
1.5	Perception of USA and China in ASEAN	19
1.6	Skewness Diagram Scoring System	20
1.7	Skewness Diagram Result	21
1.8	ASEAN in a snapshot	22
1.9	FDI in ASEAN's infrastructure	24
1.10	Comparative Infrastructure FDI in ASEAN (2018-2022, US$ million)	25

1.11 Sector-based FDI concentration in ASEAN by USA & China 26
3.1 Number of Chinese Maritime Militia Vessels in the South China Sea (2021–2022) 54
4.1 US FONOPs in the South China Sea (2018–2023) 65

Maps

1.1 BRI Projects' Map in ASEAN 27
3.1 Map of the South China Sea featuring China's nine-dash line 52

Acknowledgements

This book would not have been possible without the contributions of the distinguished speakers of the ASEAN Conference 2024 and without the unwavering support from Commodore R. S. Vasan IN (Retd), Director General of Chennai Centre for China Studies (C3S) & Regional Director, National Maritime Foundation, Tamil Nadu (NMF-TN) and Dr Manoharan N, Director, Centre for East Asian Studies (CEAS), Christ (Deemed to be) University, Bangalore. My sincerest admiration and thanks go to all the authors for submitting works of rigorous research and cooperating throughout the publication process.

Commodore Vasan granted me complete autonomy to plan and execute the conference, what more could I have asked for? I am extremely indebted and proud to have worked under his mentorship, he was a colossal pillar of strength in all my endeavours and always a source of boundless inspiration. He encouraged and entrusted me to take on the editorial reins of this book, honoured to have had that trust. On the other hand, Professor Manoharan, another rock of unwavering strength and optimism in my pursuits, is proud to call me his student. The conference was a massive success chiefly because of the unrelenting support we received from him and CEAS. He has always been accommodative of all our suggestions and was perpetually prepared to pitch in and help us out, whenever and wherever we needed his support.

In progression, I would like to once again express immense gratitude to Commodore R.S. Vasan, Director General, C3S and others including Col

R. Hariharan and Dr Indira Ravindran, distinguished members of C3S for reviewing the scholarly works of the conference speakers. Their input greatly aided in enhancing the quality of the papers and the book.

Many many thanks to Mr Ashwin Dhanabalan, Co-Coordinator C3S-CEAS ASEAN Conference and Project Associate & Senior Research Affiliate, CEAS for bearing with my incessant requests, marathon messages and for taking care of the conference logistics and more. I am overwhelmed with gratitude for the support extended by Ms Sapna Elsa Abraham, Senior Research Officer, C3S, who has been the constant pillar of support throughout the conduct of the conference and beyond, a crucial catalyst who nudged me to embark on this editing project. Further, I would like to thank my colleagues, Ms Madhumitha R. and Ms Annunthra Rangan, research officers of Chennai Centre for China Studies (C3S) for their invaluable support in organising the conference. Ms Madhumitha for being my non-stop emotional manager and cheerleader and Ms Annunthra, my personal photographer, thank you team for making this an unforgettable experience.

Abbreviations and Acronyms

ADMM-Plus	ASEAN Defence Ministers' Meeting-Plus
AFTA	ASEAN Free Trade Area
AOIP	ASEAN Outlook on the Indo-Pacific
ARF	ASEAN Regional Forum
ASEAN	Association of Southeast Asian Nations
AUKUS	Australia-United Kingdom-United States
BRI	Belt and Road Initiative
CCG	China Coast Guard
COC	Code of Conduct
EAS	East Asia Summit
ECS	East China Sea
EEZ	Exclusive Economic Zone
FDI	Foreign Direct Investment
FONOP	Freedom of Navigation Operations
FTA	Free Trade Agreement
HADR	Humanitarian Assistance and Disaster Relief
IFC-IOR	Information Fusion Centre-Indian Ocean Region
IPEF	Indo-Pacific Economic Framework
IPMDA	Indo-Pacific Partnership for Maritime Domain Awareness
IPOI	Indo-Pacific Oceans Initiative
MILAN	Mid-Planning Conference for Multilateral Naval Exercise

MPAC	Master Plan on ASEAN Connectivity
PLA	People's Liberation Army
PLAN	People's Liberation Army Navy
QUAD	Quadrilateral Security Dialogue
RCEP	Regional Comprehensive Economic Partnership
SCS	South China Sea
SCSPI	South China Sea Strategic Situation Probing Initiative
SLBM	Submarine-Launched Ballistic Missile
SSBN	Ballistic Missile Submarines
VINBAX	Viet Nam-India Bilateral Army Exercise
UNCLOS	United Nations Convention on the Law of the Sea
UUV	Uncrewed Underwater Vehicles/Unmanned Underwater Vehicles
XLUUV	Extra Large Unmanned Underwater Vehicle

China's Geo-Economic Inroads in Southeast Asia

1

East Asia & China's (Geo-economic) Footprint in Southeast Asia: ASEAN Centrality?

Dharish David and Abhisek Kumar Pandey

Abstract

This study examines the evolving geopolitical dynamics in the Indo-Pacific region and their implications for the Association of Southeast Asian Nations (ASEAN), with a focus on the challenges posed by the Quadrilateral Security Dialogue (Quad) and China's assertive regional policies, as well as India's role and impact in shaping the regional order. The analysis suggests that ASEAN's centrality could be at risk if the Quad or China unilaterally shape regional dynamics without due consideration of ASEAN's strategic interests, potentially escalating economic and security vulnerabilities within the bloc. The study will employ a comprehensive methodology, encompassing an in-depth analysis of investment, trade, infrastructure investment, and other security and economic relations of ASEAN with the US and China, as well as an examination of international negotiations and frameworks such as the Belt and Road Initiative (BRI), the Quad, and the Indo-Pacific strategy to provide a holistic understanding of the evolving geopolitical landscape in the region. The findings emphasise the significance of continued engagement and nuanced diplomacy by ASEAN in the face of an increasingly complex and contested geopolitical arena. This analysis foregrounds an ASEAN-centric perspective, a logical choice given the organisation's core aspiration of regional centrality. This research approach differs from understanding the region solely through the lens of great power rivalries to rather using a data-driven analysis of ASEAN's economic relations and investment patterns to develop an ASEAN-centric framework and findings.

Keywords: Global power dynamics, regional stability, economic, trade and security relations, AOIP (ASEAN Outlook on the Indo-Pacific), QUAD, China.

Introduction

In 2022, the ASEAN Defense Ministers Meeting Plus (ADMM-Plus) and broader diplomatic and economic initiatives led by the Association of Southeast Asian Nations (ASEAN) have set the stage for an in-depth analysis of the potential impact of the Quad's ascent and other Indo-Pacific strategies on ASEAN's central role (ASEAN Secretariat, 2020; MINDEF, 2023). This study delves into the concept of ASEAN centrality enshrined in the ASEAN Charter and underscores its significance in the evolving Indo-Pacific landscape. Furthermore, it examines ASEAN's adaptation to the shifting dynamics, including internal deliberations on fortifying its own Indo-Pacific approach. The ASEAN Outlook on the Indo-Pacific (AOIP) is highlighted as a pivotal framework that could act as a buffer between the Quad and China, averting direct confrontation and alleviating security and economic concerns for ASEAN member states.

The paper recognises that the ASEAN Outlook on the Indo-Pacific (AOIP) has faced criticism for its lack of clarity and the need for more precise expression to remain pertinent. ASEAN's cohesiveness is also being tested by internal issues, notably the political crisis in Myanmar, which poses a risk to the group's solidarity and its capacity to maintain its central position. The study emphasises the critical role of ASEAN's economic prowess and its ability to foster cooperation, especially through initiatives like the Regional Comprehensive Economic Partnership (RCEP), in preserving its influence amidst the dynamic and increasingly polarised Indo-Pacific region. Moreover, China's escalating engagement in the Indo-Pacific, characterised by its economic clout, infrastructure investments, and military advancements, has profound consequences for ASEAN and its member nations. The strategic activities of other key regional actors, including the United States, Japan, and India, also play a substantial role in shaping ASEAN's strategic environment and are integral to the discourse (Miller, 2023a).

This work will seek to explore the geopolitical dynamics of the Indo-Pacific region, focusing on the economic strategies of China and Japan and their impact on the ASEAN (ASEAN Secretariat, 2020). It raises critical questions about the nature of China's assertive economic influence, often likened to a harder form of checkbook diplomacy, and whether it supersedes Japan's approach in the region. The paper examines the implications of this geo-economic competition on ASEAN's interests and centrality, questioning whether the rivalry benefits the bloc or undermines its unity and influence. It also considers the role of specific Chinese initiatives, such as the Mekong project, in contributing to the sustainable development of the involved countries and the broader sub-region. Additionally, the paper delves into the economic convergences between India and ASEAN and seeks to define an optimal strategy for India's economic engagement to remain significant in ASEAN's policy considerations.

Furthermore, it is important to understand the broader strategic landscape, including the rise of the Quadrilateral Security Dialogue (Quad)—comprising the United States, Japan, India, and Australia—and its potential effects on ASEAN's central role in regional geopolitics (Smith, 2021). It discusses the ASEAN Outlook on the Indo-Pacific (AOIP) as a strategic framework that could potentially mediate tensions between the Quad and China, thereby reducing the risk of direct conflict and safeguarding the interests of ASEAN member states. Despite the AOIP's potential, the paper acknowledges the need for more precise articulation to ensure its continued relevance. It also highlights internal challenges, such as the political crisis in Myanmar, which poses a threat to ASEAN's unity and centrality. The paper concludes by emphasising the importance of ASEAN's economic collaboration, particularly through agreements like the RCEP, in maintaining its influence during a time of significant geopolitical shifts in the Indo-Pacific region (ASEAN Secretariat, 2016).

Who dominates FDI in the ASEAN?

China's economic presence across the globe, including in the ASEAN region, is frequently viewed as dominant due to its substantial economic capabilities. Yet, an analysis of Foreign Direct Investment (FDI) data over recent years paints a nuanced picture. Despite common perceptions, FDI figures do not support the notion of China's dominance in this area. In fact, the United States has consistently led in FDI contributions to ASEAN, being the top investor from 2019 to 2022, with the exception of 2018 when its FDI was notably lower (UNCTAD, 2021). The disruption of supply chains following the COVID-19 pandemic marked a shift in narrative, with China increasing its FDI to the region. However, China's investment levels have not reached the scale of the United States' contributions. It's important to note that ASEAN countries themselves are significant investors within the bloc, with intra-ASEAN FDI ranking as the second-highest source of investment since 2020.

Referencing Figure 1.1, which illustrates the steady growth in FDI from the top 10 investing countries over the past five years, it becomes clear that ASEAN is a focal point of investment interest not only for the USA and China but also for other nations such as South Korea, Japan, Singapore, the United Kingdom, the Netherlands, and more. The diverse interest from many large numbers of countries in investing in the region may contribute to the impression that ASEAN is becoming an increasingly attractive destination for international investment. This trend underscores the strategic economic importance of ASEAN on the global stage and highlights the competitive investment landscape within the region.

Who is dominant among the ASEAN member states?

As of 2023, ASEAN is composed of 10 member states, and while there have been discussions about East Timor's potential membership, as per last update, it has not yet been formally admitted as the 11th member state. ASEAN often presents a united stance on various issues and policies, but national interests can sometimes lead to divergent priorities among member states. When examining the distribution of FDI on a country-by-country basis, China's role as a significant investor in Southeast Asia becomes evident, particularly when looking at data from 2012 to 2021 in terms of percentage of investment.

China has established a substantial investment presence in several ASEAN countries, including Brunei, Malaysia, Laos, and Cambodia,

Figure 1.1: FDI in ASEAN by source countries (USD million)

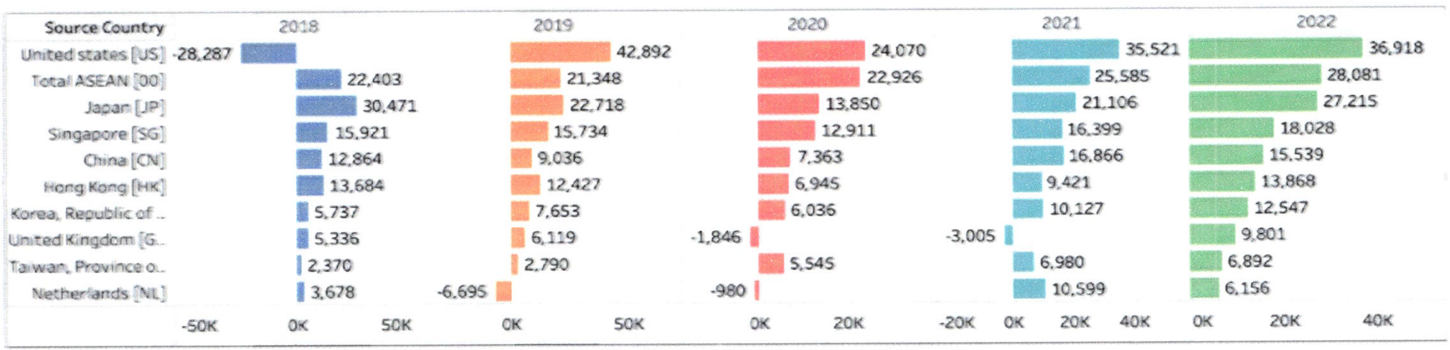

Source: ASEAN Stats Data 2023.

where Chinese investment has been significant and sometimes linked to concerns about over development, such as the so-called 'ghost towns' in Malaysia. Singapore is notable not only as a recipient of investment but also as a major source of FDI within the region. Other ASEAN nations like the Philippines, Indonesia, and Myanmar also show varying levels of investment from China, with the Philippines recently taking a more assertive stance in the Indo-Pacific. It is important to note that while China is a key player, the United States has also maintained a strong investment presence in the region, particularly in the post-COVID period, although not to the same magnitude as China's investment in South Asia (HFAC GOP, 2022) compared to China's economic influence in Southeast Asia (Bader, 2005; Kurlantzick, 2024; Pal, 2021).

Table 1.1: Cumulative FDI into ASEAN member states 2012-2021

ASEAN Member States	Top FDI Investors	Top Investors % of total investment into host country
Brunei	China	93.60%
Thailand	Japan	38.80%
Malaysia	China	28.50%
Singapore	United States	26.80%
Laos	China	25.20%
Cambodia	China	24.40%
Vietnam	South Korea	22.90%
Philippines	China	20.20%
Indonesia	China	20%
Myanmar	China	15.20%

Source: ASEAN Stats Data Portal 2023.

Who are the leading FDI Investors in ASEAN countries?

The trade dynamics within the ASEAN region have become increasingly complex, particularly in light of the strategic competition between the U.S. and China for dominance in the Indo-Pacific, as well as the implementation of the RCEP, the world's largest Free Trade Agreement (FTA). According to the data presented in Figure 1.2, which outlines the top 5 export destinations for ASEAN member states from 2018 to 2022, China stands out as a significant export destination for countries like Singapore and Indonesia, which have consistently exported a substantial percentage of their goods to China, excluding exports to Taiwan and Hong Kong. Other ASEAN members, including Vietnam, Brunei, Thailand, and Malaysia, have also maintained strong export relationships with China, securing a top 5 position in terms of export destinations over the past five years. The importance of intra-ASEAN trade is also highlighted, with Laos, for example, exporting primarily to Thailand, and Singapore and Indonesia being among the top 5 export markets for several other ASEAN member states (Bibbudatta, 2021).

This intricate web of trade relationships underscores the strategic economic importance of both intra-ASEAN trade and the region's trade with major global economies like China. The data suggests that while China has a significant trade presence in the ASEAN region, the trade relationships are multifaceted, with ASEAN countries engaging in substantial trade both within the bloc and with other major trading partners (Bader, 2005). The RCEP agreement, which includes ASEAN member states along with China and other regional economies, is likely to further influence these trade dynamics, potentially enhancing the economic integration within the region and with key partners. The intricate trade relationships within ASEAN and with major economies like China reflect the region's strategic position in the global trade landscape and the diverse economic interests of its member states.

In 2022, ASEAN nations heavily relied on China for their import needs, with China being the largest import partner for countries like Singapore, Indonesia, Malaysia, Cambodia, Vietnam, Myanmar, Philippines, and Thailand (ASEAN Secretariat, n.d.). This dependency is underscored by China accounting for approximately 25 per cent of these countries' imports, as depicted in Figure 1.3. While intra-ASEAN trade has shown signs of growth, other factors such as exclusive agreements, geographical proximity, and cultural ties also play a crucial role in shaping trade patterns. For instance, Laos's significant import reliance on Thailand highlights the complex interplay of these factors. To mitigate ASEAN's import dependency on China, enhancing intra-ASEAN trade through greater vertical integration

Figure 1.2: Top 5 Export Destinations (% share in value in export for ASEAN Member States (2018-2022)

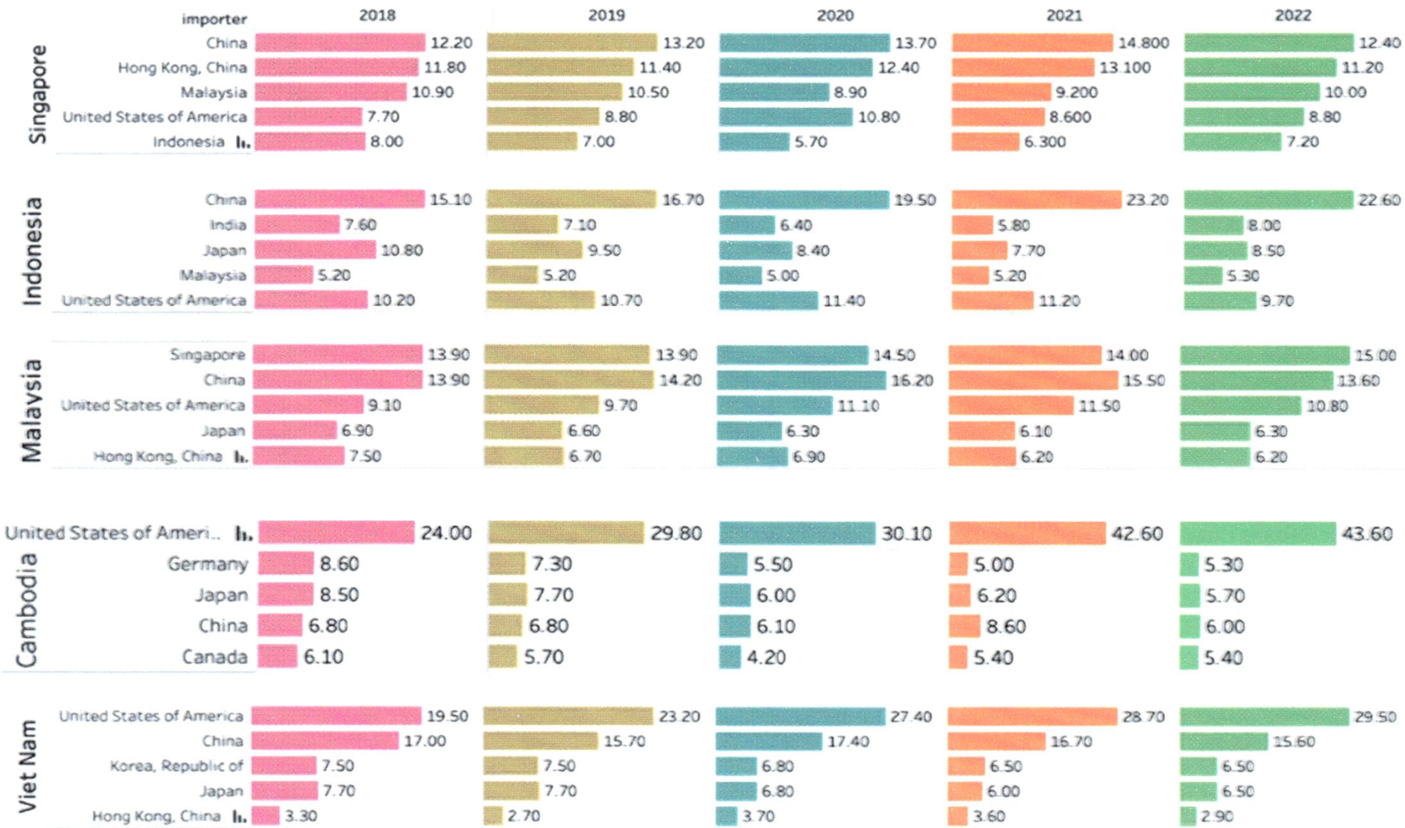

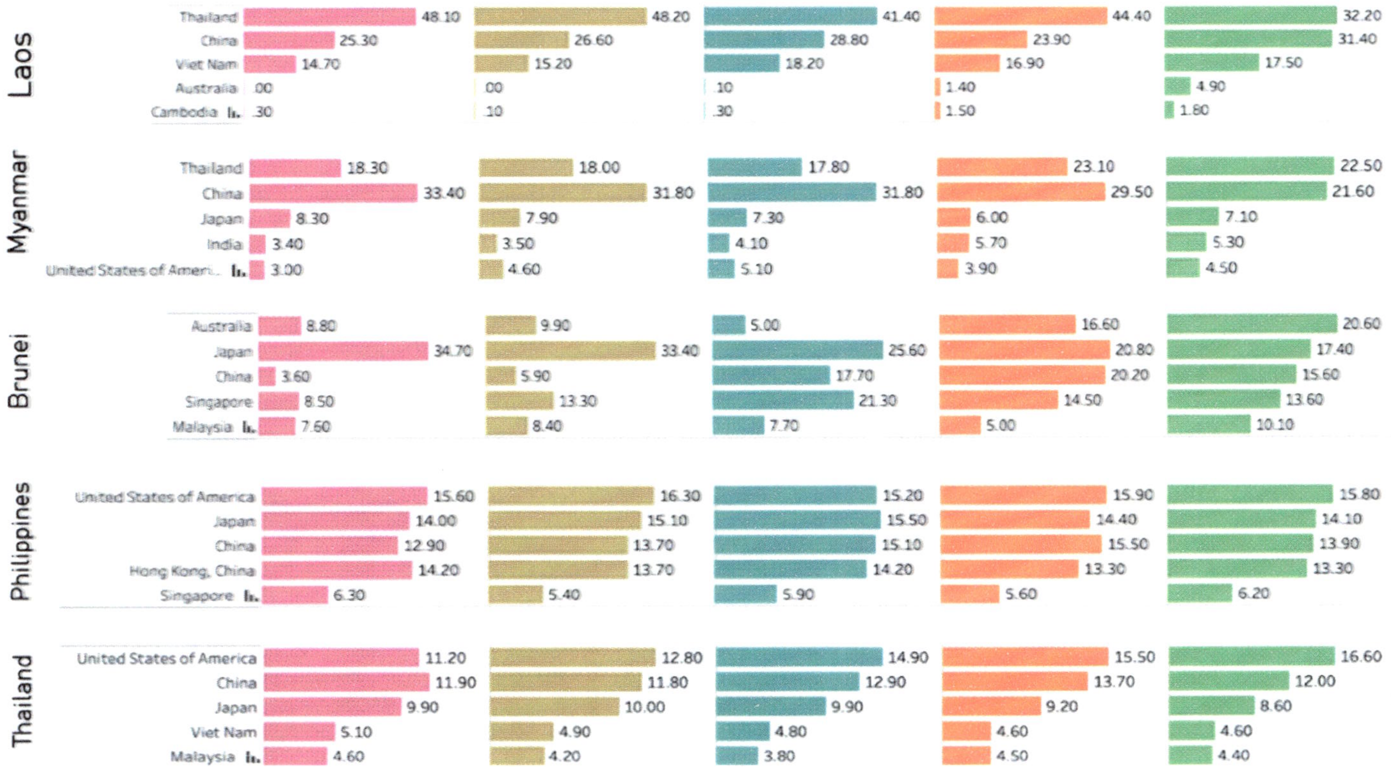

Source: Author's calculations from ASEAN Stats Data Portal 2023.

Figure 1.3: Top 5 Import Destination and % share in value in import for ASEAN Member States (2018-2022)

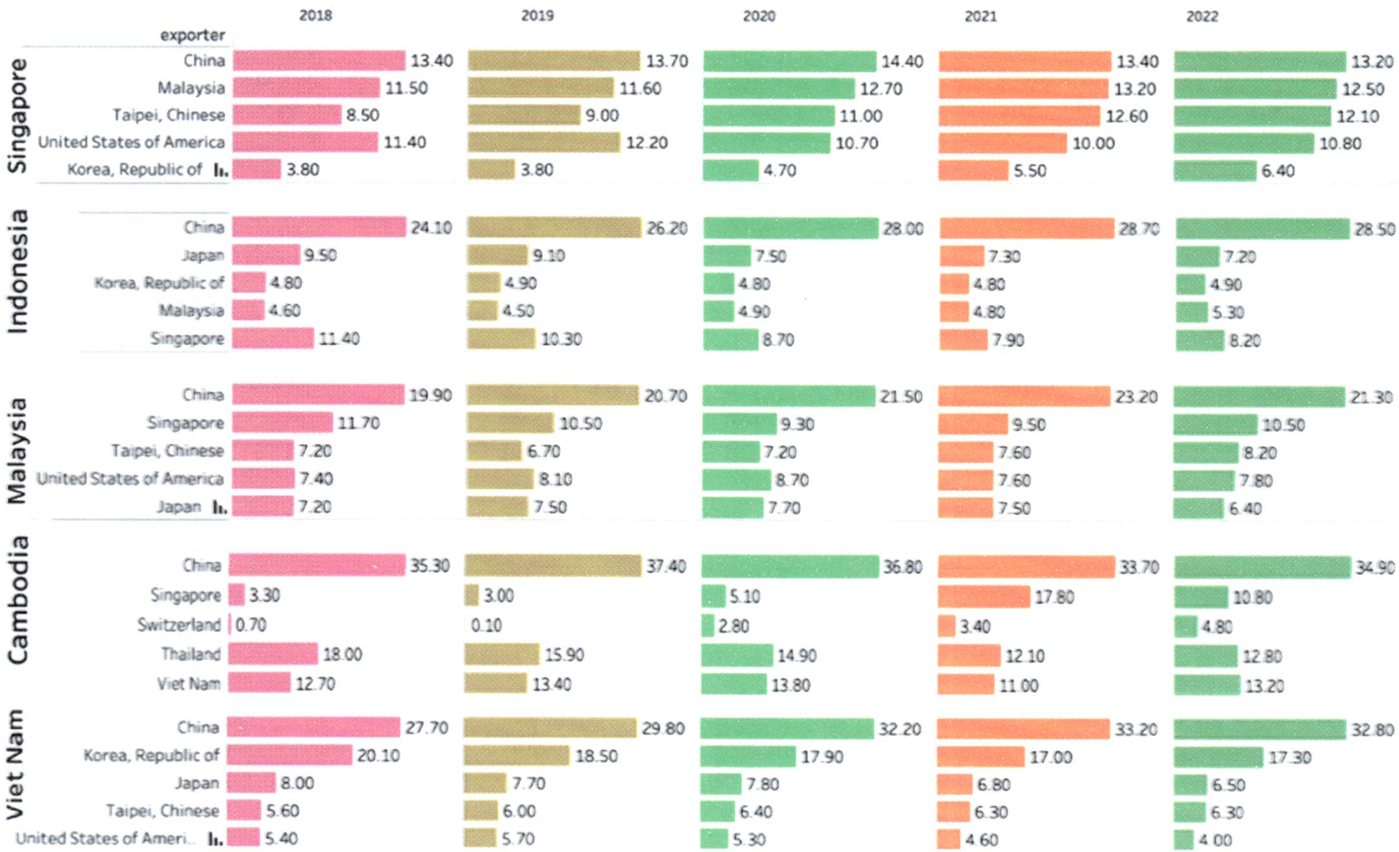

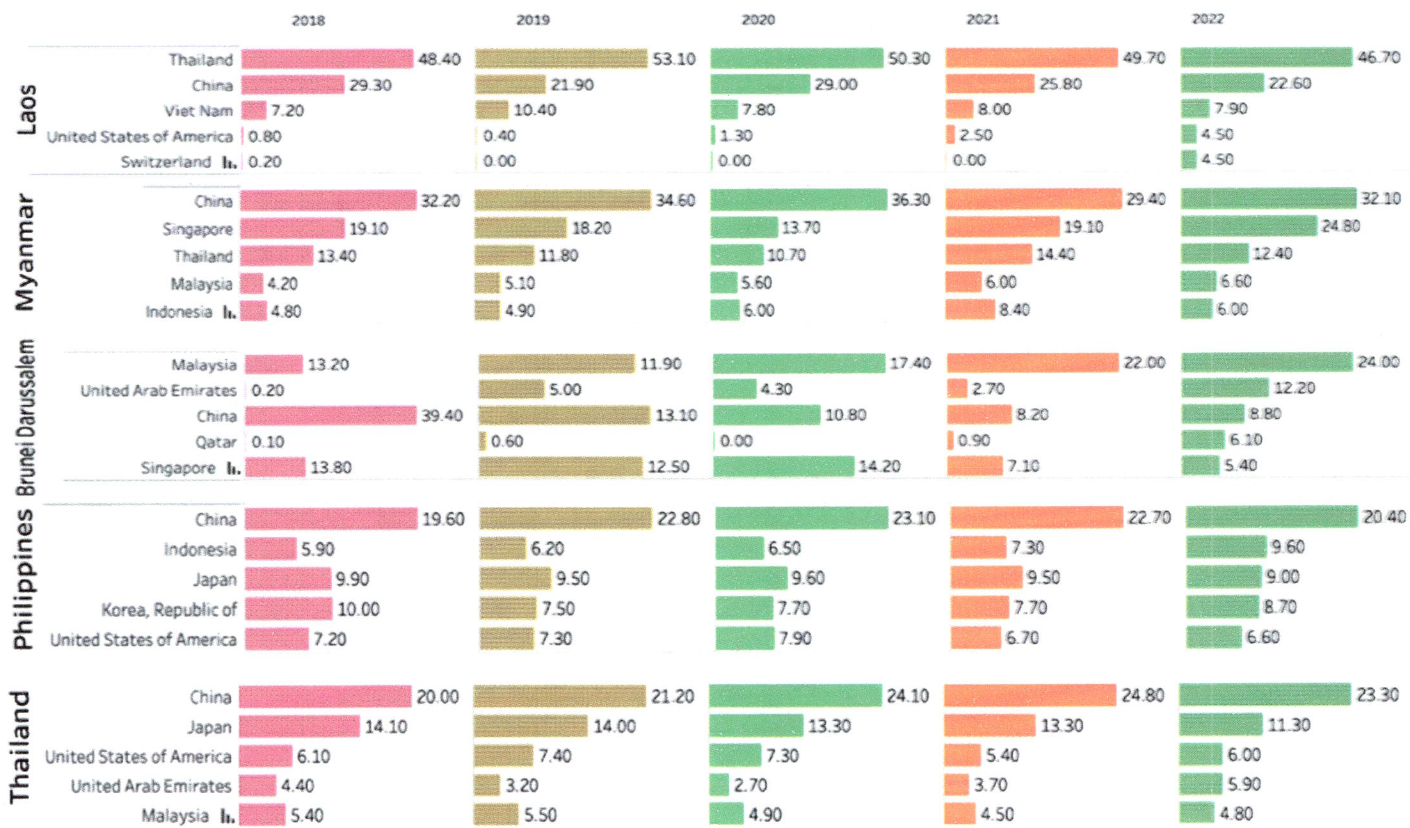

Source: Author's calculations from ASEAN Stats Data Portal 2023.

and connectivity is essential. However, achieving a reduction in dependency on China for imports will require substantial efforts to strengthen the economic ties and infrastructure within ASEAN member states (Paterson, 2022).

Table 1.2, derived from Figures 1.2 and 1.3, encapsulates the primary import and export partners for ASEAN member states in 2022, revealing a significant economic pattern reminiscent of Japan's historical development trajectory. This table illustrates ASEAN countries' efforts to diversify their import sources beyond traditional partners, including from developing nations, while aiming to increase their exports to the United States. Simultaneously, it highlights the substantial reliance of these countries on China for their import needs, with China being the predominant source of imports for Singapore, Indonesia, Malaysia, Cambodia, Vietnam, Myanmar, the Philippines, and Thailand. This scenario underscores China's substantial role as an exporter to the ASEAN region, indicating its pivotal position in the economic landscape of East Asia.

Table 1.2: Top importer/exporter of ASEAN member states (% holding)

Country	Importer	Importer's % share in import	Exporter	Exporter's % share in import
Cambodia	United States	43.6	China	34.8
Indonesia	China	22.6	China	28.5
Malaysia	Singapore	15	China	21.3
Vietnam	United States	29.5	China	32.8
Philippines	United States	15.8	China	20.2
Singapore	China	12.4	China	13.2
Laos	Thailand	32.2	Thailand	46.7
Myanmar	Thailand	22.5	China	32.1
Thailand	United States	16.6	China	23.3
Brunei	Australia	20.6	Malaysia	24

Source: ASEAN Stats Data Portal 2023.

Who dominates with regard to trade with ASEAN?

The trade dynamics within ASEAN are characterised by significant intra-regional trade, which surpasses ASEAN's trade with external partners.

According to the provided data, the export and import figures between the USA and China to ASEAN countries are closely matched, with only a 0.01 per cent difference in exports. However, there is a substantial gap in imports from ASEAN to both the USA and China for the years 2020-2022, indicating that China is also becoming an important export market for ASEAN nations.

Table 1.3: ASEAN export-import by World, ASEAN, China, USA (2020-2022)

ASEAN Export to:	2020		2021		2022	
WORLD	1393.76	100%	1716.99	100%	1956.23	100%
ASEAN	298.33	21.40%	370.68	21.59%	446.79	28.84%
China	218.07	15.65%	282.42	16.45%	291.01	14.88%
USA	212.10	15.22%	257.22	14.98%	290.94	14.87%
ASEAN Import from:	**2020**		**2021**		**2022**	
WORLD	1268.29	100%	1621.30	100%	1883.80	100%
ASEAN	298.61	23.54%	386.67	23.85%	431.63	22.91%
China	268.10	21.14%	339.32	20.93%	407.01	21.61%
USA	97.50	7.69%	109.11	6.73%	129.45	6.87%

Source: ASEAN Stats Data Portal 2023.

In the broader context of the Indo-Pacific region, ASEAN is actively engaged in various international economic arrangements, including the RCEP and the Indo-Pacific Economic Framework (IPEF), while not participating in the QUAD. RCEP, which includes ASEAN members, is driven by economic interests and aims to strengthen regional integration, with China playing a significant role (CFR, 2023). The Quad, consisting of the USA, India, Japan, and Australia, focuses on security concerns and aims to ensure a free and open Indo-Pacific, countering China's assertiveness, particularly in the South China Sea (Miller, 2023b). Despite not being a part of the Quad, ASEAN's centrality in the region is emphasised by Quad members, highlighting the importance of ASEAN's role in maintaining regional stability (Conelly, 2022). The IPEF includes India, Japan, South

Korea, New Zealand, the USA, and seven ASEAN countries, excluding Cambodia, Myanmar, and Laos. It is seen as an economic arm of the Quad and aims to enhance economic relations among its members and other Indo-Pacific countries (Saha, 2022). ASEAN's approach to these arrangements reflects a strategy of balancing power and maintaining a cautious stance to avoid disrupting the regional balance, which is crucial for ASEAN's strategic interests (Iwamoto, 2021; Parameswaran, 2023).

In summary, ASEAN's trade is dominated by significant intra-regional trade, with China emerging as a key export market for ASEAN. The region's engagement in RCEP and IPEF, along with its nuanced relationship with the Quad, illustrates ASEAN's strategic positioning and its efforts to balance economic and security interests in the Indo-Pacific.

What is the image of China and the USA in ASEAN recently?

A recent shift in public opinion towards China is evident in Southeast Asia. Following a period of perceived US favorability (2020-2023), 2024 survey data suggests a reversal in sentiment. China has emerged as the prevailing choice (50.5 per cent), surpassing the US. This finding does not surprise us, as this aligns with previous observations in countries with large Muslim populations, such as Indonesia, Malaysia, and Laos. These countries have exhibited a historical trend of closer alignment with China, potentially due to several factors. One explanation could be China's substantial investments in infrastructure projects through the Belt and Road Initiative (BRI) within these economies. Additionally, the ongoing Israel-Palestine conflict may have contributed to dissatisfaction with the US's perceived stance. The formation of the RCEP free trade agreement, with China as a key member, could further solidify regional economic ties with China. Conversely, the US-led IPEF has yet to offer comparable economic incentives (Stromseth, 2019).

China's Belt and Road Initiative (BRI) is a key element of its strategy to achieve global dominance, with both geopolitical and economic objectives. The BRI aims to facilitate the flow of goods, investment, and people and has been successful in boosting China's domestic economy and outward investment. Despite criticisms regarding debt sustainability and lack of

Figure 1.4: Arrangements in Indo-Pacific

Regional Arrangement	Regional Comprehensive Economic Partnership (RCEP)	Quadrilateral Security Dialogue (QUAD)	Indo-Pacific Economic Framework (IPEF)
Overview	•30% of global GDP •World's largest FTA •Asia Pacific countries cooperating for pure economic reasons	•40% of Global GDP, 22% of all Indo- Pacific FDI stocks •Free and open Indo-Pacific •No ASEAN member, accepts ASEAN's centrality in the region	•14 % of Global GDP •Not an FTA agreement •Trade, Supply Chain, Clean Economy & Fair economy. •Alternative to China based supply chain
Composition	10 ASEAN + 5 G20 Singapore, Malaysia, Indonesia, Myanmar, Thailand, Cambodia, Viet Nam, Brunei, Laos, Philippines, China, New Zealand, Australia, Japan, South Korea	Australia, India, Japan, United States	7 ASEAN + 7 non- ASEAN Brunei Darussalam, Indonesia, Malaysia, Philippines, Singapore, Thailand, and Viet Nam, Australia, Fiji, India, Japan, Republic of Korea, New Zealand, United States
Pillars	Negotiations for investment under the RCEP will cover the four pillars of •Promotion, •Protection •facilitation and •liberalization of trade	•maintain and strengthen stability in the Indo-Pacific (security) •Sustainable development of the region •Democratic values and uphold rule of law	IPEF began discussion of future negotiations on the following pillars: •Trade, •Supply Chains, •Clean Energy, Decarbonization, & Infrastructure, •Tax and Anti-Corruption
Aim	Creating liberal, facilitative, and competitive investment environment in the region.	promoting stability, resilience and prosperity in the Indo-Pacific	contribute to cooperation, stability, prosperity, development, and peace within the region
Relation with China	China is a key player with high interest and high influence.	Counter to China's influence and dominance in the region (security alternative)	Counter to China's economic and trade dominance in the region (economic alternative)
Relation with ASEAN	ASEAN's initiative, aggressively negotiated and stays open to include India, which opted out in last stretch	ASEAN does not overtly reject or accept QUAD. Survey on ASEAN-QUAD cooperation says 69% view the Quad as beneficial for region, just 10% fear that Quad will force ASEAN countries to choose sides, and 7% are afraid that ASEAN-Quad cooperation will provoke China	ASEAN is a member, and many ASEAN members including Singapore endorsed it to be beneficial and complementing ASEAN efforts.

transparency, the BRI reflects the complexity of Chinese foreign policy and the influence of domestic interests.

The ASEAN prioritises fostering close political, economic, and cultural cooperation among its member states. This necessitates robust infrastructure development to stimulate economic growth through enhanced investment, competitiveness, and regional and global connectivity.

China's Belt and Road Initiative (BRI) emerged as a promising avenue for achieving this objective. Indonesia, ASEAN's largest economy, embraced the BRI and developed Jakarta-Badung high-speed rail project under its umbrella which became operational in 2023. There are several high-profile projects in progress. The BRI is not without its financial and political challenges, there has been the suspension of many projects as well. However, the region jointly perceives BRI as a positive initiative in the region. Further solidifying their stance, in 2019 ASEAN-China Joint Statement aimed to synergise the Master Plan on ASEAN Connectivity (MPAC) 2025 with the BRI. This suggests a collective ASEAN acceptance of the BRI's potential benefits for the region, potentially overlooking its criticisms.

The evolving geopolitical landscape, particularly the escalating tensions between China and the United States, has heightened the strategic importance of ASEAN for China. Foreign Minister Wang Yi's initial overseas trip upon reappointment, encompassing Southeast Asian nations (Singapore, Malaysia, and Cambodia), underscores this strategic significance. As the US-China rivalry intensifies, Southeast Asia's rich endowment of critical minerals, including nickel—essential for China's green technology and electric vehicle ambitions, further amplifies its importance.

The United States has for very long acted as a guarantor of world peace and security, and Asia Pacific and ASEAN do not remain any exception to that. The United States aspires to play a key role in the security of the region. U.S.-ASEAN relations encompass a broad range of cooperative endeavours. A pivotal moment occurred at the 3rd ASEAN-US Summit in Kuala Lumpur (November 2015), where leaders elevated the dialogue to a strategic level. The 5th ASEAN-US Summit in Manila (2017) further solidified this partnership, commemorating the 40th anniversary of ASEAN-US dialogue relations. Throughout 2017, various activities marked this milestone, including U.S. Vice President Mike Pence's visit to the ASEAN Secretariat in April 2017.

The United States maintains active engagement in ASEAN's political-security architecture through participation in key forums. These include the ASEAN Regional Forum (ARF), the ASEAN Defence Ministers' Meeting-Plus (ADMM-Plus), and the East Asia Summit (EAS). These engagements foster discussions on shared interests in maritime security, cybersecurity, and countering transnational crime.

In summary, ASEAN's view of the USA and China has remained nuanced. China remains a dominant influence in the region (He, 2023). The BRI is a central part of China's strategy, with long-term goals that extend beyond immediate economic gains, despite facing criticism for its potential drawbacks (The Economist, 2023).

Figure 1.5: Perception of USA and China in ASEAN

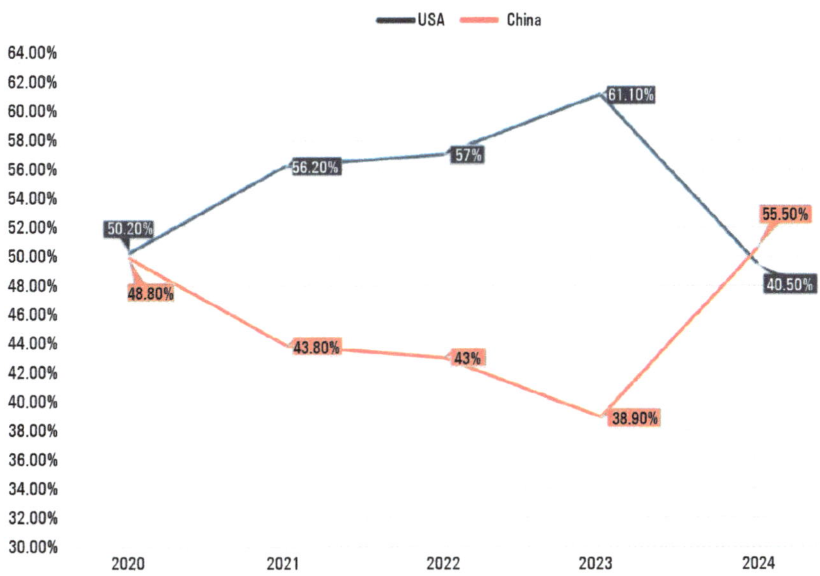

Source: ISEAS Yusof Ishak Institute (2023/42 'Southeast Asian Views on the United States–Perceptions Versus Objective Reality' by Lee Sue-Ann).

Discussion: Navigating the Tides–Economic and Security Alignments in the Indo-Pacific

The Indo-Pacific region's alignment with major global powers, China and the United States, is analysed through a qualitative scoring system ranging from 0 to 10, based on trade, investment, security agreements, and public statements. Scores towards the lower end indicate a stronger alignment with China, while scores near the top reflect a closer alignment with the United States. This system reveals that smaller Indo-Pacific nations tend to align more closely with China, attributed to its significant economic and increasing security influence in the region. Notable exceptions are the Philippines, which maintains a close security alliance with the U.S. amidst maritime tensions with China, and Singapore, which has strong economic ties with both superpowers. Larger countries like Indonesia and Thailand demonstrate a balanced approach, engaging economically with both while carefully managing diplomatic relations. Myanmar's middle-range score, despite its political closeness to China, suggests a pragmatic foreign policy balancing between security and economic interests (Busbarat, *et al.*, 2023).

Figure 1.6: Skewness Diagram Scoring System

Score Range	Description	Explanation	Description	Explanation
0-2	Strong economic alignment with China	Extensive economic projects, investments, and trade agreements with China	Strong security alignment with China	Strong defence and security cooperation with China, potentially aligning in regional security matters
3-4	Moderate economic alignment with China	Significant economic ties with China, but also engaged in economic partnerships with other nations	Moderate security alignment with China	Engaged in security dialogues with China but maintaining a level of independence
5-6	Neutral economic stance	Balance economic engagements with both China and Quad nations	Neutral security stance	Balancing security interests without strong alignment, avoiding significant military commitments

7-8	Moderate economic alignment with Quad	Strong economic cooperation with Quad nations with notable project and trade agreement	Moderate security alignment with Quad	Active participation in security dialogues joint exercise regional security cooperation with Quad nations
9-10	Strong economic alignment with Quad	Extensive economic ties, joint ventures, and trade agreements with Quad nations	Strong security alignment with Quad	Deep security ties with Quad nations potentially participating in joint defence initiatives

The study recognises the limitations of its preliminary scoring system and the need for a more nuanced analysis that could include factors like cultural ties and historical legacies. It underscores the importance of understanding the diverse economic and security alignments within the Indo-Pacific, as these hold key insights into the region's shifting power dynamics and potential areas of conflict. The findings emphasise the challenge for smaller nations in balancing economic interdependence with security needs amidst complex geopolitical rivalries. Future research is encouraged to explore the intricate factors influencing countries' alignment decisions and their broader implications for regional stability and cooperation.

Figure 1.7: Skewness Diagram Result

China Skew	Score Range	Economic	Security
	0-2		
	3-4	Cambodia, Malaysia, Laos, Brunei	Brunei, Cambodia, Vietnam
	5-6	Myanmar, Philippines, Indonesia, Thailand, and Vietnam	Indonesia, Laos, Myanmar, Thailand
	7-8	Singapore	Singapore
Quad Skew	9-10		Philippines

Source: Author's own analysis, assessment, and visualisation.

ASEAN's Evolution: Navigating Geopolitical Shifts and Charting a Future Path

ASEAN has come a long way since its inception during the Cold War era, evolving from a fragile alliance of five nations to a ten-member bloc poised to welcome an eleventh. Overcoming early regional conflicts and internal challenges, ASEAN has made significant strides in economic integration, particularly with the establishment of the ASEAN Free Trade Area (AFTA). The financial crisis of 1997 served as a turning point, prompting the bloc to strengthen its legal framework and deepen cooperation towards a unified ASEAN Community, encompassing political, economic, and social integration. Today, ASEAN faces contemporary challenges such as maritime disputes and climate change, yet it continues to play a pivotal role in fostering regional dialogue and maintaining a rules-based order. With "ASEAN Vision 2025," the bloc envisions a future of connectivity, digital innovation, and sustainability, ensuring its relevance amid global changes.

Figure 1.8: ASEAN in a snapshot

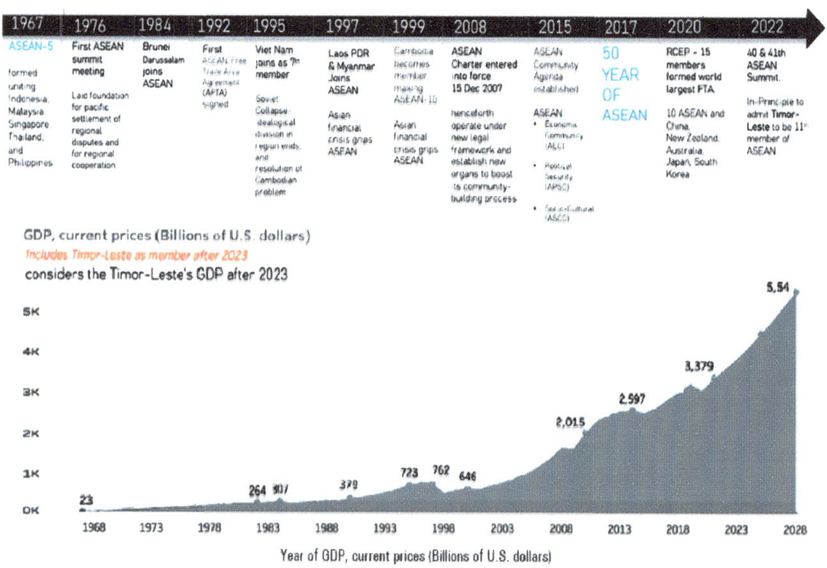

Source: ASEAN Main Portal & International Monetary Fund (IMF).

In contrast to the South Asian Association for Regional Cooperation (SAARC), which has struggled with political and economic disparities among its members, ASEAN has emerged as a more dynamic and effective model of regional cooperation. The historical influence of colonialism, as well as the significant roles of India and China, have shaped the geopolitical landscape of the region. The emergence of the Quad, comprising the U.S., Japan, Australia, and India, has introduced new dynamics, with ASEAN countries benefiting from the cooperative efforts of these powers. ASEAN's success is largely due to its consensus-based approach to conflict management, a strategy that has proven less effective in SAARC. Looking forward, ASEAN's Vision 2045 aims to further integration and connectivity, addressing modern challenges such as digitalisation, environmental sustainability, and socio-economic disparities (Wiadnyana, 2023). The bloc's diplomatic skill in managing complex relationships with major global powers will be key to its continued success and influence in the region.

China's Belt and Road Initiative: Impact on Global Infrastructure Investment

China's Belt and Road Initiative (BRI), initiated in 2013, is a global development strategy aimed at enhancing regional connectivity and embracing a brighter economic future by reviving the historical Silk Road. The BRI focuses on building extensive infrastructure, such as ports, roads, and railways, to facilitate trade and assert China's economic influence worldwide (Habib & Viktor, 2017). The initiative's appeal, particularly to developing nations, stems from its emphasis on speed and cost-effectiveness, offering a more rapid development pace than the traditionally high-quality, high-cost infrastructure projects typically associated with Japan, such as the Delhi Metro project funded through Official Development Assistance (ODA).

The BRI's reach extends from ASEAN to Africa and Latin America, serving China's strategic interests, including securing resources, expanding export markets, and enhancing its global economic presence (Cai, 2017). Despite these ambitions, the BRI has attracted scrutiny over concerns such as the risk of debt dependency for participating countries, non-transparent lending practices, and the potential for creating neo-colonial relationships (CGD, 2018). In contrast, the United States has shown a relative lack of engagement in global infrastructure investment, particularly in ASEAN, prompting questions about its strategic intentions and competitive stance in

Figure 1.9: FDI in ASEAN's infrastructure (USD million)

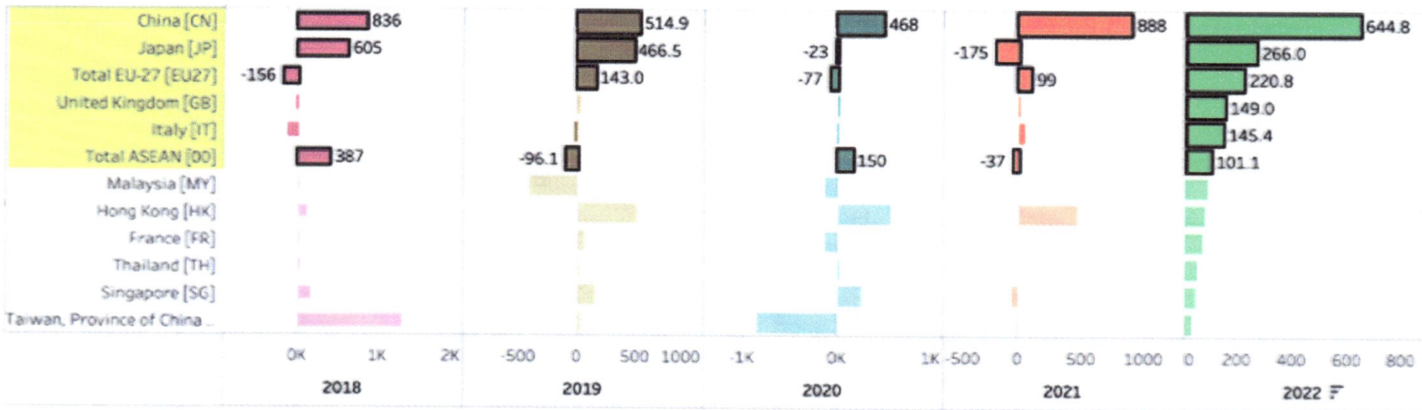

Source: ASEAN Data Stats portal 2023 and as visualised by the authors.

this arena. The BRI's emergence challenges established Western dominance in global infrastructure and presents an alternative vision for economic connectivity. However, the long-term effects on international relations and power dynamics are yet to be fully understood, necessitating further research to evaluate the BRI's impact, risks, and benefits within the global political economy.

Figure 1.10: Comparative Infrastructure FDI in ASEAN (2018-2022, US$ million)

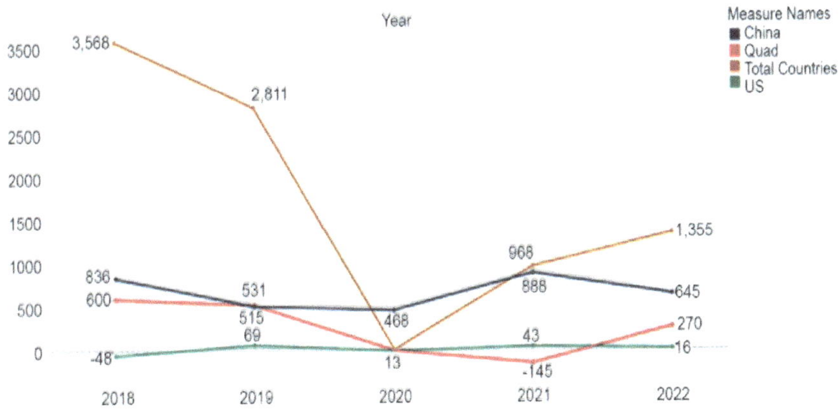

Source: ASEAN Data Stats portal 2023 and as visualised by the authors.

As of 2023, the United States and China are employing distinct strategies to exert influence in the Indo-Pacific region. The US is focusing on nearshoring policies to reduce supply chain vulnerabilities, emphasising financial investments in ASEAN to develop it as a manufacturing and financial hub that could serve as an alternative to China (US Department of State, 2024). This strategy is partly driven by concerns over strategic dependence on China, leading to increased investments in domestic chip production and other security-sensitive industries. Meanwhile, China continues to expand its Belt and Road Initiative (BRI), pouring significant investment into ASEAN's infrastructure, including energy, rail and ports. The strategic placement of these investments, often in areas of geopolitical tension, suggests that they may serve dual purposes, extending beyond mere economic development.

Figure 1.11: Sector-based FDI concentration in ASEAN by USA & China

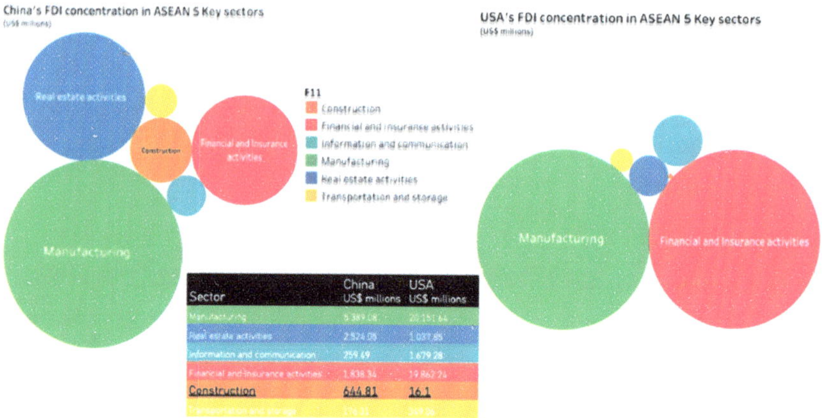

Sector	China US$ millions	USA US$ millions
Manufacturing	5,389.08	20,151.64
Real estate activities	2,524.05	1,037.85
Information and communication	259.69	1,679.28
Financial and insurance activities	1,838.34	19,862.24
Construction	644.81	16.1
Transportation and storage	[illegible]	[illegible]

Source: Author's calculation and visualisation of ASEAN Data Stats Portal 2023.

This study adopts the size and sectoral composition of investing countries as a proxy for their influence and area of interest in ASEAN. While this approach offers valuable insights, it presents a primarily quantitative assessment. Future research could be enriched by incorporating qualitative factors that delve deeper into the motivations and strategies behind investment decisions in ASEAN. This would provide a more nuanced understanding of investment dynamics within the region.

India, while not the primary focus of either the US or China, has manufacturing capabilities that are attracting attention. The escalating competition between the US and China in ASEAN presents challenges for the Quad—comprising India, Japan, Australia, and the US—which aims to foster regional cooperation (Ayres, 2018). Key questions remain unanswered: Will India align with one of the superpowers or pursue an independent path? Can China's infrastructure-focused strategy ensure long-term economic and environmental sustainability? And how will the complex interactions of trade, investment, and security influence regional stability, as well as the strategic interests of India and the Quad? These questions highlight the need for in-depth analysis and strategic dialogue to navigate the future of the Indo-Pacific region.

Map 1.1: BRI Projects' Map in ASEAN

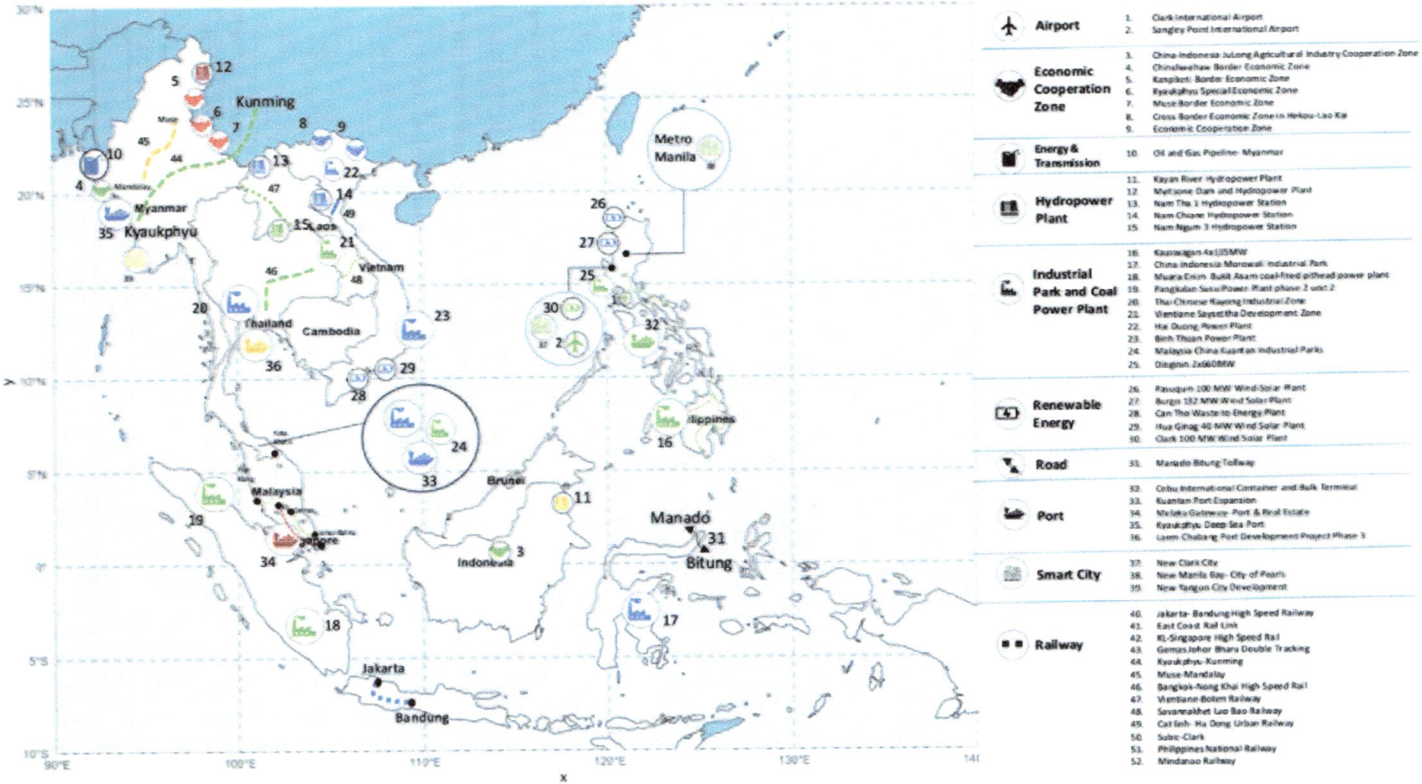

Source: Park, A. F., Sejko, D., & Tritto, A. (2020). *The Hong Kong University of Science and Technology IEMS.*

The Rising Economic Clout of ASEAN and India: Demographics, Growth and Future Projections

The economic futures of ASEAN, India, and China, when analysed through data spanning from 2012 to 2022 with projections up to 2032, present a compelling narrative of growth and potential. ASEAN's population, currently at 670 million, is poised for significant growth, potentially outpacing India's 1.4 billion population peak. This demographic shift heralds a burgeoning consumer market and a boost in both production and consumption demand. Economically, ASEAN's GDP stands at USD 3.3 trillion, slightly trailing India's USD 3.53 trillion, yet forecasts suggest that by 2032, the two economies may converge in size. While China's economy is expected to double to USD 12 trillion, its growth rate is projected to decelerate, positioning ASEAN and India as fastest-growing economies.

India, approaching its demographic zenith, possesses a substantial workforce and consumer market, which could be leveraged to fuel economic expansion. However, India's intricate political environment could pose challenges, contrasting with ASEAN's emphasis on economic partnerships and relative political stability. The ability of India to navigate its internal complexities will be crucial in capitalising on its demographic dividend. In essence, ASEAN is on track to emerge as a significant economic player, with its strategic focus on growth and collaboration. India, with its unique strengths and obstacles, is also set to make substantial economic strides. The forthcoming decade will be pivotal as these Asian powerhouses delineate their economic paths, influencing the regional and global economic landscape.

Table 1.4: Comparison of historic and projection trends for USA, China, ASEAN and India

Country/ region	Year	Population (million)	Population peak	GDP Current (USD Tn)	GDP per capita (USD)	Average GDP growth rate (%)
USA	2012	313.71	2080	16.26	51,857	1.9 (2003-12)
	2022	338		25.44	76,329	1.9
	2032	358		32+	107,397	
China	2012	1,347.35	2084	8.12	6,300	10.56 (2003-12)
	2022	1,444.05		17.72	12,341	3

	2032	1,629		23+	20,930	
ASEAN	2012	613	2060-70	2.48	2,061	6.4 (2003-12)
	2022	679		3.63	5,000	5.2
	2032	732		7.32	9,290	
India	2012	1,210.16	2060-70	1.83	1,434	6.97 (2003-12)
	2022	1,400.55		3.42	2,558	7.2
	2032	1,531		8.62	5,100	

Source: IMF & World Economic Outlook (October 2023), World Bank Development Indicators, United Nations Population Fund.

The paper, while covering a lot of ground covering ASEAN-centric economic analysis, points to several potential areas for future research including a qualitative comparison of investments by different powers in ASEAN nations, an in-depth study on whether the "debt-trap" issue from China's BRI has impacted ASEAN countries, research into broader public perceptions of BRI across the region, and clarifying the significance of the "ASEAN 2025" and "ASEAN 2045" integration milestones.

Conclusion

In conclusion, the evolving economic and geopolitical dynamics in the Indo-Pacific region, particularly involving ASEAN, India, China, and the United States, are shaping a new era of global influence and economic potential. The data indicates that ASEAN is poised for substantial growth, driven by its favourable demographics and focus on economic cooperation. India's demographic advantage and expanding consumer base also position it as a significant player in the region. China's Belt and Road Initiative (BRI) and the U.S.'s nearshoring policies reflect distinctive strategies to exert influence in the region. The rise of BRI challenges traditional Western dominance in global infrastructure investment, while the US's nearshoring policies seek to mitigate supply chain vulnerabilities. The competition between the US and China in ASEAN poses challenges for regional cooperation, particularly for the Quad. Unanswered questions remain about India's alignment with major powers, the long-term sustainability of China's infrastructure-heavy approach, and the broader implications of these trends on regional stability and cooperation. Further research is essential to critically assess these trends, evaluate potential risks and benefits, and understand their broader implications for the evolving global political economy.

References

ASEAN Secretariat. (n.d.). *ASEAN-China Economic Relations.* Retrieved 17 February 2024, from https://asean.org/our-communities/economic-community/integration-with-global- economy/asean-china-economic-relation/

ASEAN Secretariat. (2016). *Regional Comprehensive Economic Partnership (RCEP).* https://asean.org/regional-comprehensive-economic-partnership-rcep/

ASEAN Secretariat. (2020). *ASEAN Outlook on the Indo-Pacific.* https://asean.org/asean2020/wp-content/uploads/2021/01/ASEAN-Outlook-on-the-Indo-Pacific_FINAL_22062019.pdf

Ayres, A. (2018, November 20). The Quad and the Free and Open Indo-Pacific. *Council on Foreign Relations.* https://www.cfr.org/blog/quad-and-free-and-open-indo-pacific

Bader, J. (2005, September 6). China's Role in East Asia: Now and the Future. *The Brookings Institution.* https://www.brookings.edu/articles/chinas-role-in-east-asia-now-and-the-future/

Bibbudatta, A. (2021, April 15). Chinas Relationship with ASEAN: An Explainer. *Observer Research Foundation.* https://www.orfonline.org/research/china-relationship-asean-explainer

Busbarat, Pongphisoot, CAMBA, A., INAS, F., & PO, S. (2023). *How Has China's Belt and Road Initiative Impacted Southeast Asian Countries*? Carnegie Endowment for International Peace. https://carnegieendowment.org/2023/12/05/how-has-china-s-belt-and-road-initiative-impacted-southeast-asian-countries-pub-91170

Cai, P. (2017, March 22). Understanding China's Belt and Road Initiative. *The Lowy Institute.* https://www.lowyinstitute.org/publications/understanding-china-s-belt-road-initiative

CFR. (2023, September 18). What is ASEAN? Backgrounder. *Council on Foreign Relations.* https://www.cfr.org/backgrounder/what-asean

CGD. (2018, March 4). China's Belt and Road Initiative Heightens Debt Risks in Eight Countries, Points to Need for Better Lending Practices. *Centre for Global Development.* https://www.cgdev.org/article/chinas-belt-and-road-initiative-heightens-debt-risks-eight-countries-points-need-better

Conelly, A. (2022, June 9). The often-overlooked meaning of 'ASEAN centrality.' *International Institute for Strategic Studies (IISS).* https://www.iiss.org/en/online-analysis/online-analysis/2022/06/the-often-overlooked-meaning-of-asean-centrality/

Habib, B., & Viktor, K. (2017, May 16). The Belt and Road Initiative: China's vision for globalisation, Beijing-style. *The Conversation.* https://theconversation.com/the-belt-and-road- initiative-chinas-vision-for-globalisation-beijing-style-77705

He, H. (2023, July 15). China eyes ASEAN trade ties, but members fear 'geopolitical trap as US also seeks regional influence. *The South China Morning Post.* https://www.scmp.com/economy/china-economy/article/3227769/china-eyes-asean-trade-ties-members-fear-geopolitical-trap-us-also-seeks-regional-influence

HFAC GOP. (2022, November 14). China Regional Snapshot: South Asia. *House Foreign Affairs Committee GOP.* https://foreignaffairs.house.gov/china-snapshot-project-south-asia/

Iwamoto, K. (2021, June 21). *ASEAN defends its Indo-Pacific 'centrality' between Quad and China.* Nikkei Asia. https://asia.nikkei.com/Spotlight/Asia-Insight/ASEAN-defends-its-Indo-Pacific-centrality-between-Quad-and-China

Kurlantzick, J. (2024, January 9). *Chinas Public Image Actually Getting Worse. Council on Foreign Relations.* https://www.cfr.org/blog/chinas-public-image-actually-getting-worse

Miller, M. C. (2023a, August 21). The Quad and ASEAN Must Learn to Work Together. *Council on Foreign Relations.* https://www.cfr.org/article/quad-and-asean-must-learn-work-together

Miller, M. C. (2023b, August 22). Cooperation Between ASEAN and the Quad is Critical for Indo-Pacific Stability. *Council on Foreign Relations.* https://www.cfr.org/blog/cooperation-between-asean-and-quad-critical-indo-pacific-stability

MINDEF. (2023, November 16). ADMM-Plus Defence Ministers Commit to Multilateral Cooperation for a Peaceful and Stable Region at 10th ADMM-Plus. https://www.mindef.gov.sg/web/portal/mindef/news-and-events/latest-releases/article-detail/2023/November/16nov23_nr

Pal, D. (2021). Chinas Influence in South Asia: Vulnerabilities and Resilience in Four Countries Carnegie Endowment for International Peace. https://carnegieendowment.org/2021/10/13/china-s-influence-in-south-asia-vulnerabilities-and-resilience-in-four-countries-pub-85552

Parameswaran, P. (2023, December 21). Southeast Asia and US-China Competition: Contours, Realities, and Implications for the Indo-Pacific. *Wilson Center.* https://www.wilsoncenter.org/article/southeast-asia-and-us-china-competition-contours-

Park, A. F., Sejko, D., & Tritto, A. (2020). https://iems.ust.hk/publications/reports/uob-bri-overview. *The Hong Kong University of Science and Technology IEMS.* https://iems.ust.hk/publications/reports/uob-bri-overview

Paterson, S. (2022, February 22). To ease ASEAN's import dependency, strengthen intra-ASEAN trade. *Hinrich Foundation.* https://www.hinrichfoundation.com/research/article/ftas/aseans-import-dependency-intra-asean-trade/

Saha, P. (2022, June 25). The Indo-Pacific Economic Framework (IPEF): An ASEAN perspective.

Observer Research Foundation. https://www.orfonline.org/research/the-indo-pacific-economic-framework

Smith, S. (2021). The Quad in the Indo-Pacific: What to Know. *Council on Foreign Relations.* https://www.cfr.org/in-brief/quad-indo-pacific-what-know

Stromseth, J. (2019, October). Don't make us choose: Southeast Asia in the throes of US-China rivalry. *The Brookings Institution.* https://www.brookings.edu/articles/dont-make-us-choose-southeast-asia-in-the-throes-of-us-china-rivalry/

The Economist. (2023, June 15). America is losing ground in Asian trade. *The Economist.* https://www.economist.com/finance-and-economics/2023/06/15/america-is-losing-ground-in-asian-trade

UNCTAD. (2021). *ASEAN Investment Report 2021.* https://investasean.asean.org/files/upload/ASEAN%20Investment%20Report%202020-2021.pdf

US Department of State. (2024). Indo-Pacific Strategy. *US Department of State.* https://www.state.gov/subjects/indo-pacific-strategy/

Wiadnyana, N. (2023, November 29). A look at ASEAN's new Vision 2045. *UNU-MERIT.* https://www.merit.unu.edu/asean-new-vision-2045/

China's Maritime Influence in the ASEAN Region & Prospects for India-ASEAN Collaboration

2

Chinese Maritime Strategy and its Impact on Southeast Asia & Beyond: A Philippine Perspective

RAdm Rommel Jude G Ong AFP (Retd)

Abstract

The paper looks at China's aim to secure its access to resources and markets and protect its east coast, by expanding its maritime forces northward, eastward, and southward. Its actions in the South China Sea affect the Philippines' energy, food, and territorial security. The paper describes the Philippine response, which includes asserting its sovereign rights, enhancing its defence and maritime capacity, and engaging in bilateral and multilateral cooperation with other countries. It also notes the initiatives undertaken by the Philippines to counter China's maritime ambition, such as reviving the PH-US alliance, exploring trilateral cooperation with the US and Japan, developing bilateral defence agreements with Australia, Japan, and France, and involvement in various ASEAN-led mechanisms. The paper also suggests that India could be a potential strategic partner for the Philippines and ASEAN in the Indo-Pacific region. The Philippines needs to adopt a comprehensive and coherent maritime strategy that balances its national interests and regional obligations and leverages its diplomatic, defence, and economic tools to manage the South China Sea dispute. It should also work towards strengthening its domestic institutions, enhance its maritime security capabilities, diversify its security and economic partners, and continue to promote a rules-based order in the region.

Key Words: China, Philippines, Maritime Security, Maritime Strategy.

Background

China's Maritime Strategy

China's maritime strategy supports two geo-economic imperatives: (1) to ensure access to resources and markets across the globe, and (2) to protect its vulnerable east coast. To secure its access to the global supply chain, it has three discernible axes of advance. First is the northward axis, which radiated towards the unfrozen Arctic Ocean and Europe. Second is the eastward axis, which projects beyond its so-called 'first island chain' and radiates towards the mid-Pacific and the Americas. The third is a southward axis that traverses the South China Sea and moves towards the Indian Ocean, thence the Middle East, Africa, and the Mediterranean Ocean.

To achieve such an objective, China has modernised the PLA-Navy (PLA-N), allowing it to gradually execute far-sea operations beyond its maritime comfort zone. In fact, a study by the US Congressional Research Service conducted a few years ago indicated that PLA-Navy (PLA-N) has surpassed the US Navy in the total number of combatant vessels since 2015. This is due to well-placed investments in state-owned shipyards, which have been rolling out destroyers and frigates annually at an alarming rate. In comparison, the US Navy has been suffering a decline in the number of combatant vessels in its inventory and severely lacks operational shipyards stateside that can compete with its Chinese counterpart. Of course, the expansion of the Chinese Coast Guard (CCG), and the mobilisation of its Peoples Armed Forces Maritime Militia (PAFMM) should not be discounted.

China also needs to secure its eastern coastline; and the ten provinces that generate a substantial percentage of the country's Gross Domestic Product (GDP) (Textor, 2022). These dovetails with the vision of the late Admiral Liu Huaqing, the former Commander in Chief of the PLA Navy (1982-1988) and later Vice-Chairman of the Central Military Commission (1993-1998). He asserted that "the Chinese Navy should exert effective control of the seas within the First Island Chain, [comprising] the Aleutians, the Kurils, the Japanese archipelago, the Ryukyus, Taiwan, the Philippine archipelago, and the Greater Sunda Islands, [as well as the] Second Island Chain [that is] composed of the Bonins, the Marianas, Guam, and the Palau group" (Huang, 1994, p. 18). Consistent with Admiral Huaqing's concept, China is compelled to attain the following four (4) objectives:

(i) Sea control over their 'nine-dash line,' which includes the North. East, South China Sea and the airspace above it.

(ii) Sustained presence in key features such as the Senkaku Islands, Panatag Shoal, James Shoal, and Natuna Islands.

(iii) Ensure continued access to SLOCS such as the Bashi Channel and Luzon Strait, Mindoro Strait, Balabac Strait and Malacca Strait.

(iv) Influence, Engagement, or Cooptation of Key Countries that fall astride the so-called 'nine-dash line,' such as North Korea, South Korea, Japan, Taiwan, the Philippines, Brunei, and Malaysia.

To achieve the first three objectives, it has developed the requisite hard power, which is based on the operational synergy of its PLA-N, CCG, and PAFMM vessels operating from fixed bases in Hainan, as well as the Paracel and Spratlys Island Groups. These maritime forces are employed by China to assert sea control over the South China Sea, shadow transiting US and other foreign navies, and coerce coastal states in the region from accessing its own exclusive economic zone. To achieve the fourth objective, China uses its sharp power which involves the use of manipulative policies to influence and undermine the political system of another country. In Southeast Asia, it has leveraged its economic prowess to enmesh ASEAN member states under its sphere and influence its political and policy elites to align with Beijing. China needs to keep the surrounding countries friendly or destabilised to keep its weak, dissuade the formation of an alliance against its interests, and most importantly prevent the US from asserting its presence in the region.

Impact on Philippine Maritime Interests

China's maritime ambition manifests itself through excessive territorial claims and the use of coercive actions within the Philippines' exclusive economic zone. Its 'gray zone tactics' using its CCG and PAFMM vessels, have imposed existential challenges to the country's energy and food security. On April 4, 2022, a CCG vessel harassed the Geo Coral, and the Mariska G, these were two survey vessels contracted by PXP Energy Corp to conduct a seismic survey at Service Contract 75 (SC 75) and Service Contract 72 (SC 72) in the vicinity of Reed Bank. Located about 60 miles off the western coast of Palawan, it is supposed to contain up to 4.6 trillion cubic feet (TCF) of gas. This is comparable to the 3.4 TCF of gas reserves available in Malampaya, which is projected to run out of gas by 2027.

China has 'blockaded' Scarborough Shoal. This is a traditional area for artisanal fishing among Filipinos based along the coast of northwest Luzon. Last September 22, 2023, the CCG installed a 300-meter-long barrier at the entrance to prevent Filipino fisherfolks from entering the shoal. A crew from the Philippine Coast Guard (PCG) removed a portion of the barrier on instructions from Manila, triggering a verbal tirade with China (Serquiña, 2023). In a recent incident last December 9, 2023, a Bureau of Fisheries and Aquatic Resources (BFAR) vessel was harassed by CCG and militia vessels while in the process of providing supplies to Filipino fishing boats found near the shoal. The latter used a water cannon and a long-range acoustic device (LRAD), which caused damage to the BFAR vessel's communication and navigation equipment.

Chinese activities in the Spratlys Group of Islands are geared towards expanding sea control beyond the eight isles and features it currently occupies. Around the waters of the Second Thomas Shoal, CCG and militia vessels have also imposed a 'blockade' to prevent the Philippine Navy (PN) from sustaining its outpost there; the BRP Sierra Madre, a WW2-era transport ship that was deliberately grounded in response to the occupation of Mischief Reef decades ago. The vessel is in a state of deterioration, and China is preventing efforts to repair it or replace it with an alternative platform. On November 10, 2023, China surged 38 vessels to deter the PN from resupplying BRP Sierra Madre, and used a water cannon with reckless manoeuvers to harass the PN and PCG vessels involved (Magramo & Register, 2023). In a more recent incident, last December 10, 2023, CCG and militia vessels disrupted another resupply mission, causing propulsion damage to a supply boat and structural damage to a PCG escort vessel. A second supply boat was deliberately 'rammed' by another CCG vessel; albeit there was no physical damage incurred and it was able to successfully complete its mission. Meanwhile, in other areas in the Spratlys Island Group, PAFMM vessels are being used to establish 'presence' in the unoccupied shoals and reefs that are still within the country's EEZ. On 3 December 2023, approximately 135 militia vessels swarmed inside Whitsun Reef, a feature that is located 175 nautical miles from Palawan. The vessels were observed to anchor together in a row, in a formation described by analysts as 'rafting,' to create a temporary floating outpost out at sea.

On the domestic front, there were indications that through malign influence, China might be undermining the country's national security and foreign policy posture. It was disconcerting to note the inroads made by the CPP in the telecommunications sector, among local government officials, and key provinces with strategic significance. Also, certain personalities identified to be supportive of former President Rodrigo Duterte's appeasement policy toward Beijing are still very much around and have become 'talking heads' that spout CCP-driven propaganda.

The Philippine Response

Arbitral Ruling and Current Domestic Political Posture

In the PCA ruling of July 12, 2016, the arbitral tribunal issued a unanimous award in favour of the Philippines, invalidating most of China's claims in the South China Sea and affirming the sovereign rights of the Philippines in its EEZ. It also found that China's historical rights over the South China Sea were extinguished by the Convention, that none of the features claimed by China were entitled to an exclusive economic zone or continental shelf, and that China violated the Philippines' rights and the Convention by interfering with its fishing and oil exploration activities, constructing artificial islands, and endangering the marine environment (PCA, 2016). To this date, the arbitral ruling has been supported by the following states: United States, Australia, Austria, Belgium, Canada, Czech Republic, Denmark, European Union, Finland, France, Germany,

Greece, India, Ireland, Italy, Japan, the Netherlands, New Zealand, Poland, Romania, Slovakia, Spain, Sweden, and the United Kingdom.

Before his formal assumption, then President-elect Ferdinand "Bongbong" Marcos Jr. has expressed the intention to assert the country's sovereign rights by upholding the country's claim in the West Philippine Sea. He has also stated that he would not compromise the country's sovereignty in any way (Cervantes, 2022). In his first State of the Nation Address (SONA) in 2022, he emphasised that "[he] will not preside over any process that will abandon even one square inch of the territory of the Republic of the Philippines to any foreign power." He also committed to protecting the Philippine territory and working towards developing consensus with other nations on areas of disagreement (CNN, 2022). This sets the tone for Marcos' foreign policy position and national security agenda.

Defence and Maritime Security Capacity-building to Enforce the PCA Ruling

With the looming resolution of the country's domestic security challenges, the Armed Forces of the Philippines (AFP) is transitioning from counterinsurgency to territorial defence. On the part of the Philippine Navy (PN), it opted years ago for an asymmetric solution to counteract the PLA-Navy surface fleet operating in the West Philippine Sea (WPS).

Before 2023 ends, the Philippine Marine Corps (PMC) expects the initial delivery of the Bhramos anti-ship missile batteries. Once operational, it should provide a 290 km buffer along the entire west coast of the Philippine archipelago, to mitigate against China's superior surface fleet. On the other hand, the Israeli-made Shaldag fast attack crafts, along with the earlier acquisition of multi-purpose attack crafts, are supposed to enhance the PN's ability to control at least some, if not all of the seven archipelagic straits within the Philippine archipelago. These straits include Luzon Strait, Mindoro Strait, Balabac Strait, Sibutu Strait, Basilan Strait, Surigao Strait and San Bernardino Strait. It provides access to the adjacent seas around the country, which could become a major vulnerability if it remains unguarded. These are just a partial glimpse of the AFP's modernisation program, which is currently under review by the Department of National Defense.

Maritime Presence at the WPS

The Philippine Coast Guard (PCG) bears the brunt of countering China's gray zone operations in the WPS. A few years ago, Tokyo provided 12 offshore patrol vessels to the PCG. These vessels are currently employed to patrol various isles and features in the Spratlys Group of Islands, and tracking the PAFMM vessels moving around the unoccupied shoals located inside the country's EEZ. It also escorts the Navy's supply boats running the blockade of CMM and PAFMM vessels that swarm around the Second Thomas Shoal, and assists Filipino fisherfolks who are being harassed by the CCG at the Scarborough Shoal.

The country's situation in the WPS has garnered international support. For instance, Japan has recently agreed to provide the country with coastal surveillance radar and five additional offshore patrol vessels for the PCG, under the new Official Security Assistance (OSA) framework (Kosuke, 2023). Germany has earlier donated to the PCG two unmanned aerial vehicles (UAV) for use in the conduct of maritime surveillance, disaster response, and reconnaissance purposes (Ylade, n.d.). On the other hand, Canada will allow the country access to its 'Dark Vessel Program,' which uses satellite technology to locate and track ships illegally fishing even if they switch off their location transmitting devices to evade monitoring and surveillance (Callar, 2023).

Countering Propaganda and Disinformation

China's coercive tactics at sea are replicated in the public opinion space as well. CCP-inspired propaganda and disinformation continue to push for the 'legitimacy' of its excessive maritime claims in the South China Sea and justify its use of grey zone tactics within the country's own EEZ. To address this, the government has adopted a transparent approach in collaboration with local media, by spotlighting Chinese coercive activities at sea, particularly in the Scarborough Shoal, Second Thomas Shoal and Whitsun Reef. In some cases, these efforts moderate the behaviour of CCG and PAFMM vessels, if their actions impose reputational costs against the CCP; in other times, China has taken a more aggressive counter-response.

Bilateral and Minilateral Approaches to Addressing Regional Security Challenges

Reviving the PH-US Alliance

President Marcos Jr. has undertaken actions to restore the security ties between the Philippines and the US. On January 19-20, the 10th PH-US Bilateral Security Dialogue (BSD) was held in Manila. This was followed on April 11, 2023, by the 3rd US-PH 2+2 Ministerial Dialogue at Washington, D.C., in 2023. These meetings covered not only security but also political and economic cooperation issues. It also provided an opportunity for both parties to reaffirm their commitment to the 1951 Mutual Defense Treaty, the 1998 Visiting Forces Agreement (VFA), and the 2014 Enhanced Defense Cooperation Agreement (EDCA). Moreover, future discussions were considered to address emerging threats in the land, sea, air, and cyber domains. On May 3, 2023, the Bilateral Defense Guidelines were agreed on by the defence departments of both countries. Among the salient points were (DOD, 2023):

(i) Conduct combined maritime activities (CMA) for maritime security and domain awareness;
(ii) Pursue trilateral and other forms of multilateral cooperation;
(iii) Sustain participation in multilateral forums such as ASEAN;
(iv) Implement the Enhanced Defense Cooperation Agreement;
(v) Conduct exercises, education, and training activities designed for defence against kinetic, space and cyberspace threats, and enhance combined planning skills;
(vi) Enhance decision-making, communication, and information-sharing protocols;
(vii) Enhance cooperation on information security, cyber defence, and cyber security; and CBRNE and counter-WMD capability.

On November 23, 2023, the Philippine Navy and Air Force conducted its first Maritime Cooperative Activity (MCA) in the West Philippine Sea with the US 7th Fleet. It provided three combatant naval vessels and three aircrafts, while the Americans brought in the littoral combat ship USS Gabrielle

Giffords, and a P-8A Poseidon aircraft (Nepomuceno, 2023). Relatedly, this was followed on November 25, 2023, by an MCA with Australia. Here, the Royal Australian Navy Frigate HMAS Toowoomba sailed with a Philippine Navy offshore patrol vessel and landed dock ship within the country's EEZ (Valente & Tuyay, 2023).

Emerging Trilateral Cooperation Regime

The idea of a trilateral cooperation among the Philippines, the US, and Japan was first explored last February, during the official visit of President Marcos to Japan (Tomacruz, 2023). Since then, the National Security Advisers (NSAs) of the three countries met last June 16, 2023, in Tokyo. Affirming their shared values and security concerns, the three agreed to enhance defence cooperation; conduct of joint naval exercises, advance defence cooperation frameworks, promote maritime domain awareness, and also address economic coercion, among others (White House, 2023). During the November visit of Japanese Prime Minister Kishida to Manila, it was reported that the possibility of a trilateral alliance might have been discussed (Heydarian, 2023). For the Philippines, such an arrangement would provide the time and space for its government to fill in diplomatic, defence, and economic gaps in the immediate term. The most compelling driver for such cooperation is a common objection to the coercive posture and excessive territorial claims by the CCP in the South China Sea. A trilateral cooperation regime among the Philippines, Japan, and the United States is a step forward in mitigating the effectiveness of China's geopolitical strategy in East Asia (Ong, 2023).

Other Bilateral Defence Cooperation Mechanisms

Outside of the PH-US alliance, the Philippines has recently concluded arrangements with other countries. For Australia, on September 8, 2023, Australian Prime Minister Anthony Albanese and President Marcos met to discuss ways to enhance existing defence and maritime security ties. This was highlighted by the signing of the Australian-Philippines Strategic Partnership agreement. The two also agreed to convene an annual defence chiefs meeting, and for Australia to run joint naval patrols with the Philippines through the South China Sea for the first time (Prime Minster Office, 2023). In the case of Japan, on November 3, 2023, Japanese Prime Minister Kishida Fumio and President Marcos Jr. agreed to expand bilateral defence cooperation to better respond to common security challenges. Specifically, both parties agreed to start a discussion on the Reciprocal Access Agreement (RAA), which allows the two militaries to train and operate in each other's country (Kosuke, 2023). Lastly, on December 2, 2203, Frances Defense Minister Sébastien Lecornu met with Defense Secretary Gilberto Teodoro. Both parties briefly touched on a possible visiting force agreement between the two militaries. But the main point was France's interest in participating in the AFP's modernisation program and the DND's Self-Reliant Defense Posture (SRDP) Program; along with intentions for deepening defence relations in the areas of maritime security, intelligence-sharing, and education and training, among others (Inquirer, 2023).

Prospects for ASEAN intervention in the South China Sea

ASEAN has to contend with three types of fears; the fear of entrapment, the fear of abandonment, and the fear of China. It hedges to avoid getting caught in the middle of the US-China rivalry. It has not publicly supported the country's arbitral award. However, there are recently approved mechanisms that offer potential relief, provided that these are managed adroitly. To begin with:

ASEAN Guidelines for Maritime Interaction (GMI)

It was adopted during the 13th ASEAN Defence Ministers Meeting in Bangkok, Thailand, on 11 July 2019. It aims "to establish comprehensive and feasible maritime conflict management measures based on confidence-building, preventive diplomacy, and peaceful management of tensions that could arise at sea" (ASEAN Defence Minister's Meeting, 2019). This pertains to international law and regional conventions including, among others, the United Nations Convention on the Law of the Sea (UNCLOS), International Regulations for Preventing Collisions at Sea

(COLREG), and CUES. Last May 10, 2023, its technical and operational parameters were approved during the 17th ASEAN Navy Chiefs Meeting (ANCM) held in the Philippines (Rita, 2023). The GMI applies to ASEAN navies and its maritime agencies on a voluntary basis. It could qualify as an alternative ASEAN-only Code of Conduct (COC). Since it is fairly recent, ASEAN member states could test and validate it in future naval exercises, and advocate for its adoption by the maritime agencies through the ADMM Expert Working Group on Maritime Security.

ASEAN Coast Guard Forum

After a few attempts to organise ASEAN's coast guard, the latest iteration, which is the ASEAN Coast Guard Forum, was convened by BAKAMLA (Indonesian Maritime Security Agency) in Bali, Indonesia, last November 2022. The forum was intended as a platform for ASEAN's coast guards and maritime agencies to collaborate and share information on various maritime security concerns. It could address the safety of navigation and communication at sea; combating transnational crime, including trafficking in illicit drugs, piracy and armed robbery at sea, and illegal arms trafficking; and conducting search and rescue operations. Moreover, this forum can potentially be a norm-setting mechanism; which sets the 'standard of behaviour' based on a rules-based international order.

ASEAN Agreement on Aeronautical and Maritime Search and Rescue Cooperation (AAMSRC)

It was published in January 2023. It replaces the 2010 ASEAN Declaration on Cooperation in Search and Rescue of Persons and Vessels in Distress at Sea, upon ratification of the former. It should foster cooperation among the member states and establish a common protocol for multilateral SAR operations. It can be socialised through the ASEAN Coast Guard Forum or the ADMM Expert Working Group on Maritime Security (EWG-MS). In either case, it can be packaged as a confidence-building measure and implemented in future search and rescue exercises involving ASEAN member states and their dialogue partners.

Nexus of Cooperation with India

Independently, or as part of the Quadrilateral Dialogue (QUAD), India could be the best fit as ASEAN's strategic partner. Its "Act East Policy" promoted "economic cooperation, cultural ties and development of a strategic relationship through continuous engagement at bilateral, regional, and multilateral levels" (Press Information Bureau, 2015). This could be complemented by the ASEAN-India Plan of Action CY 20162020; it was adopted in August 2015, and 'identified concrete initiatives and areas of cooperation along the pillars of political security, economic, and sociocultural.' In terms of defence cooperation, the Indian Navy (IN) has recently participated in the ASEAN-India Maritime Naval Exercise last 2-8 May 2023. This is a step forward, moving towards more complex naval engagements in the future. Both parties should also study the opportunities for collaboration among information-sharing centres, such as India's National Maritime Domain Awareness Centre and Singapore's Changi Information Fusion Centre. Lastly, India's robust defence industry could support the requirements of the ASEAN militaries.

Conclusion

China's maritime ambition poses an existential challenge to the Philippines. At some point, it needs to come up with a more coherent counter-strategy that balances its national interests and regional obligations and leverages its diplomatic, defence, and economic tools to protect its interests in the West Philippine Sea. This should be in tandem with acts strengthening its domestic institutions, enhancing its maritime security capabilities, diversifying its security and economic partners, and continuing to promote a rules-based order in the region.

References

Alexander Chieh-cheng Huang. *The Chinese Navy's Offshore Active Defense Strategy: Conceptualization and Implications*. Naval War College Review, Summer 1994, Vol. 47, No. 3, p. 18.

ASEAN Defence Minister's Meeting. (2019). ASEAN Defence Ministers' Meeting (ADMM) Guidelines for Maritime Interaction. In *ADMM*. https://admm.

asean.org/dmdocuments/2019_July_13th%20ADMM_Bangkok,%2011%20 July%202019_6.%20(Final)%20ADMM%20Guidelines%20for%20Maritime%20 Interaction.pdf

Catherine Valente and Francisco Tuyay. *PH, Australia begin joint naval patrol in WPS.* Manila Times. n.d. https://www.msn.com/en-ph/news/national/ph-australia-begin-joint-naval-patrol-in-wps/ar-AA1kw5nh

C. Textor. *Gross domestic product (GDP) of China 2022, by region.* Statista. May 1, 2023. https://www.statista.com/statistics/278557/gdp-of-china-by-region/

CNN Philippines. *Marcos renews pledge to defend PH territory, manage conflicts through consensus.* July 25, 2022. https://www.cnnphilippines.com/news/2022/7/25/marcos-sona-defending-ph-territory.html

Department of Defense. *Fact Sheet on U.S.-Philippines Bilateral Defense Guidelines.* May 3, 2023. https://www.defense.gov/News/Releases/Release/Article/3383607/fact-sheet-us-philippines-bilateral-defense- guidelines/

Filane Mikee Cervantes. *Marcos to invoke 2016 PCA ruling to assert territorial rights.* Philippine News Agency. May 26, 2022. https://www.pna.gov.ph/articles/ 1175254

Inquirer. PH, France begin talks on visiting forces deal—Teodoro. December 2, 2023. https://www.msn.com/en-us/news/other/ph-france-begin-talks-on-visiting-forces-deal-teodoro/ar-AA1kSDY4

Joviland Rita. *ASEAN navies approve maritime interaction guidelines*, GMA Integrated News. May 11, 2023. https://www.gmanetwork.com/news/topstories/ nation/869696/asean-navies-approve-maritime-interaction- guidelines/story/

Kathleen Magramo and Larry Register. *Philippines accuses Chinese vessels of firing water cannon on ships resupplying South China Sea military outpost.* CNN World. November 10, 2023. https://edition.cnn.com/2023/11/10/asia/south-china-sea-philippines-water-cannon-intl-hnk/index.html

Mariel Celine Serquiña. *China installs floating barrier in Scarborough Shoal—PCG*, CNN Philippines. September 4, 2023. https://www.cnnphilippines.com/ news/2023/9/24/scarborough-barrier.html

Michaela Del Callar. *Canada to boost PH maritime security in Indo Pacific—Joly.* GMA News Online. May 19, 2023. https://www.gmanetwork.com/news/ topstories/nation/870596/canada-to-boost-ph-maritime-security-in-indo-pacific-joly/story/

Permanent Court of Arbitration. PCA Press Release: *The South China Sea Arbitration* (The Republic of the Philippines v. The People's Republic of China). July 12, 2016. https://pca-cpa.org/en/news/pca-press-release-the-south-china-sea-arbitration-the-republic-of-the-philippines-v-the-peoples-republic-of-china/

Press Information Bureau. *Act East Policy,* Ministry of External Affairs, Government of India. December 23, 2015. https://pib.gov.in/newsite/PrintRelease.aspx?relid=133837

Priam Nepomuceno. *PH, US maritime patrols shadowed by Chinese ship – Brawner.* Philippine News Agency. November 23, 2023. https://www.pna.gov.ph/articles/1214268

Prime Minister Media Release. *A stronger partnership between Australia and the Philippines.* September 8, 2023. https://www.pm.gov.au/media/stronger-partnership-between-australia-and-philippines

Richard Javad Heydarian. *Japan-Philippines moving toward US-led trilateral alliance.* Asia Times. November 6, 2023. https://asiatimes.com/2023/11/japan-philippines-moving-toward-us-led-trilateral-alliance/

Rommel Ong. *Trilateral cooperation among PH, US, Japan: Acceptability, implications, impact on regional security.* Rappler. June 29, 2023. https://www.rappler.com/voices/thought-leaders/analysis-trilateral-cooperation-philippines-united-states-japan-regional-security/

Run Ylade. *Germany enhances Philippine Coast Guard's security capacity by donating unmanned aerial vehicles.* Giz. n.d. https://www.giz.de/en/worldwide/110503.html

Sofia Tomacruz. *Philippines, Japan, US trilateral partnership still in 'early stage,' says Manalo.* Rappler. May 16, 2023. https://www.rappler.com/nation/philippines-japan-united-states-trilateral-partnership-early-stage-manalo- may-2023/

Takahashi Kosuke. *Japan, Philippines Agree to Intensify Defense Cooperation.* The Diplomat. November 3, 2023. https://thediplomat.com/2023/11/japan-philippines-agree-to-intensify-defense-cooperation/

White House Briefing Room. Joint Readout of Trilateral Meeting Between the National Security Advisors of the United States, Japan, and the Philippines. June 16, 2023. https://www.whitehouse.gov/briefing-room/statements-releases/2023/06/16/joint-readout-of-trilateral-meeting-between-the-national-security-advisors-of-the-united-states-japan-and-the-philippines/

3

China's Maritime Militia in the South China Sea: Implications to ASEAN Countries' Food and Territorial Security

Nguyen Hoang Anh Thu

Abstract

As a subset of the national militia, the Chinese maritime militia plays a pivotal role in coastal defence, fishery production, intelligence gathering, support for naval operations, and enforcement of maritime territorial claims. However, its presence and activities in the contested South China Sea have become a source of concern for several ASEAN countries. This paper examines the impacts of the Chinese maritime militia's activities on the food and territorial security of these countries. Research shows that China has employed its maritime militia to advance national interests since the 1950s. Over time, the militia force has developed and grown substantially due to subsidies and support from the Chinese government. The operations of Chinese militia vessels not only contribute to the depletion of fish stocks but also interfere with the fishing rights of vessels from countries in the region. In addition, ASEAN member states have accused Chinese vessels of intruding into the disputed waters and engaging in acts of intimidation and harassment. Such actions have fostered a climate of distrust and uncertainty, thereby jeopardizing regional stability.

Key Words: Chinese Maritime Militia, ASEAN, South China Sea, Food Security, Territorial Security.

Situation in the South China Sea and China's Policies

The South China Sea stands as an important body of water connecting the Pacific Ocean and the Indian Ocean (Lalremsiami & Patnaik, 2020). It covers an area of more than three million square kilometres (Schofield, 2016). The South China Sea plays a crucial role in maritime shipping, international trade, energy exploitation, and fisheries. Thousands of ships pass through the South China Sea every day to deliver goods and link markets. Annually, USD 5.3 trillion worth of trade traverses its waters (Hui & Michael, 2017). According to the RAND Corporation, 40 per cent of the global liquefied natural gas flowed through the South China Sea in 2017 (Sacks, 2022, p. 3). Additionally, around 12 per cent of the world's total fish catch is sourced from this sea (Gnanasagaran, 2018).

The South China Sea is also one of the world's most contested areas with overlapping claims by six parties, namely China, Brunei, Malaysia, the Philippines, Taiwan, and Vietnam. These claimants rely on historical records or interpretations of international law, including the 1982 United Nations Convention on the Law of the Sea (UNCLOS), to legitimise their claims (Geraci, 2019). Poling (2022a) identifies two types of disputes related to the South China Sea: first, territorial disputes over its rocks and reefs, and second, disputes over the waters, airspace, seabed, and subsoil around the islands of the South China Sea. As of now, the aforementioned disputes have not been resolved.

In recent years, the situation in the South China Sea has deteriorated. While China's growing assertiveness has been the primary contributing factor, the actions of other relevant parties have also added complexity to the situation (Poling, 2022b). In an effort to reduce the risk of conflict and manage disputes in the South China Sea, the Association of Southeast Asian Nations (ASEAN) and China have been negotiating a Code of Conduct (COC). Despite years of negotiations, the COC has not yet been concluded (Damayanti, 2024).

China marks out approximately 90 per cent of the South China Sea as its sovereign territory using the so-called 'nine-dash line' (Strating, 2022) (see Map 3.1). Consequently, this hinders other claimant states from exercising their sovereign rights as stipulated by the UNCLOS. On July 12, 2016, the Permanent Court of Arbitration in The Hague ruled that China's nine-dash line had no legal basis (Campbell & Salidjanova, 2016). China, however, refused to participate in the arbitration and rejected the ruling (Campbell & Salidjanova, 2016, pp. 2-4). To defend its position, China has reclaimed lands, installed military structures, and increased the presence of its navy, coast guard, and maritime militia in the South China Sea (Kuok, 2019). Notably, China has adopted grey zone tactics that operate below the threshold of outright military conflict, but still enable the country to assert its maritime claims and extend its influence in the region (McLaughlin, 2022). One of the frontline operators of China's grey zone tactics has been the maritime militia. This paper examines the impact of the Chinese maritime militia's activities on the food and territorial security of ASEAN member states, particularly the claimant states in the South China Sea.

China's Maritime Militia in the South China Sea

According to Article 22 of the Law of the People's Republic of China on National Defence, the militia constitutes a component of China's armed forces alongside the People's Liberation Army and the People's Armed Police Force ('Law of the People's Republic of China on National Defence,' 1997). This law specifies that the militia undertakes responsibilities related to war preparedness, defence, and the preservation of public order ('Law of the People's Republic of China on National Defence,' 1997). Article 36 of the Military Service Law of the People's Republic of China defines the militia as "an armed organization of the masses not divorced from production" and "an assisting and reserve force for the Chinese People's Liberation Army" ('Military Service Law of the People's Republic of China,' 1984). In other words, the militia is a military auxiliary (Nguyen & Ton, 2019).

As a subset of the national militia, the maritime militia (*haishang minbing* 海上民兵) plays a pivotal role in coastal defence, fishery production, supporting naval operations, and enforcing maritime territorial claims (Yatsuzuka, 2023). In addition, several scholars discuss the involvement of China's militia force in intelligence gathering and reconnaissance (Erickson

Map 3.1: Map of the South China Sea featuring China's nine-dash line

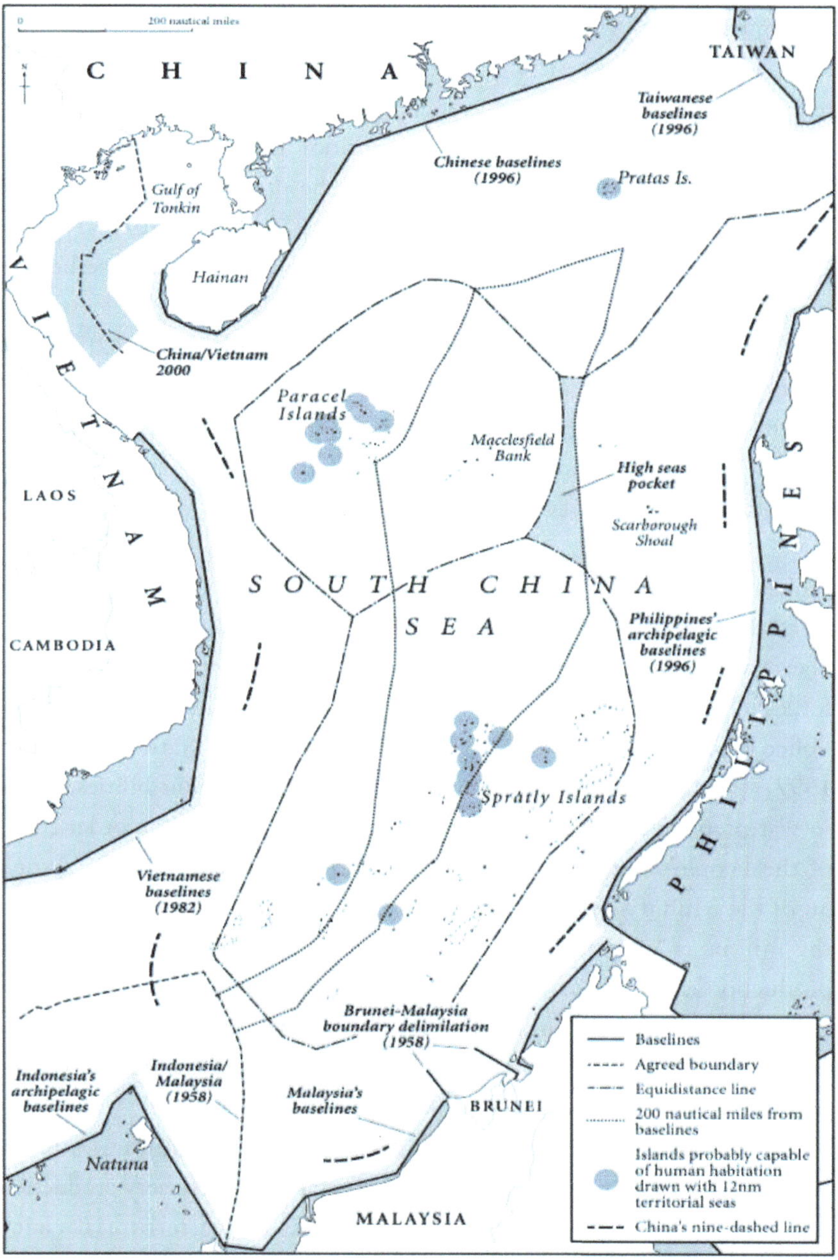

Source: Hayton, B. (2014). *The South China Sea: The Struggle for Power in Asia*. Yale University Press.

& Kennedy, 2016; Yoo & Koo, 2022). China's maritime militia is under the command of the Central Military Commission, the Provincial Military District, and regional governments (Huang & Hung, 2021). It is, however, separate from two traditional maritime forces: People's Liberation Army Navy (PLAN) and the China Coast Guard (CCG) (Luo & Panter, 2021). The maritime militia is often regarded as a "non-traditional force," an "irregular force" or "little blue men" (Erickson & Kennedy, 2015).

The use of China's maritime militia for defence purposes can be traced back to the 1950s (Hale, 2021). During that period, maritime security agencies such as the PLAN were weak and, therefore, required support from civilians (Hu, 2022). Furthermore, the concept of "People's War," which involves mobilising the entire population for national defence, has been upheld by many Chinese leaders (Hu, 2022). The Communist leader Mao Zedong emphasised that "[t]he Navy must also rely on the people; it must rely on fishermen. It must plant roots among the fishermen" (Steeds, 2022, p. 209). The People's War concept, hence, serves as a rationale for the establishment of the maritime militia. Over the years, the maritime militia has significantly contributed to a variety of tasks and operations.

Under the administration of President Xi Jinping, the frequency and scope of China's maritime militia operations have increased considerably (Miura, 2021). Significant efforts and resources have been made to train the militia force, build new vessels, and install modern equipment (McDevitt, 2016). President Xi also paid visits to fishing villages, engaging in conversations with and offering encouragement to members of the maritime militia (Baijie, 2013). In particular, during his 2013 visit to the Tanmen fishing town located in Qionghai city of Hainan Province, he told the militia members to "not only lead fishing activities but also collect oceanic information and support the construction of islands and reefs" (Zhang & Bateman, 2017, p. 290).

China's maritime militia is built out of the fishing industry. As explained in a report by the Centre for Strategic and International Studies, the maritime militia force operating in the South China Sea is composed of "professional Maritime Militia Fishing Vessels" constructed with military features and "Spratly Backbone Fishing Vessels" which are civilian fishing vessels either recruited and renovated or purpose-built to conduct military activities (Poling *et al.*, 2021, pp. 12-13). These militia vessels are equipped with advanced technologies, such as satellite navigation, communication systems, and radar (Kraska & Monti, 2015). Furthermore, the militia forces undergo military training and engage in drills with the PLAN and the CCG (Nguyen & Ton, 2019). The maritime militia of China operates mainly from 10 ports in Guangdong and Hainan Provinces (Poling *et al.*, 2021).

The central and local governments of China have allocated many different types of subsidies to support the creation and development of its maritime militia. Examples of the central government's support include fuel subsidies, vessel construction subsidies, and equipment installation subsidies, among others. Local governments of Guangdong and Hainan Provinces also provide other forms of support (Poling *et al.*, 2021, pp. 15-25).

There are no specific statistics regarding the size of China's maritime militia, however, scholars contend that China has the world's largest maritime militia (Erickson, 2017). Satellite imagery shows that hundreds of Chinese militia vessels operate in the South China Sea daily ('The Ebb and Flow of Beijing's South China Sea Militia,' 2022) (see Figure 3.1).

Figure 3.1: Number of Chinese Maritime Militia Vessels in the South China Sea (2021–2022)

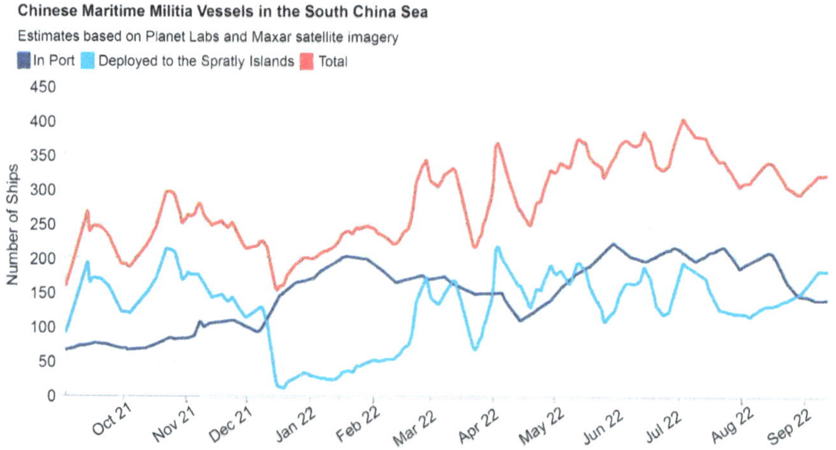

Source: 'The Ebb and Flow of Beijing's South China Sea Militia,' 2022.

Impacts on the Food Security of ASEAN Countries

Although most of the attention has been directed towards maritime territorial disputes and geopolitical rivalry, the depletion of marine resources merits more attention, due to its potential to induce food insecurity in the region, particularly among coastal communities in ASEAN countries.

The South China Sea is known as one of the world's richest marine ecosystems. Nearly 3,365 species of fish are recorded therein (Alien *et al.*, 2000). Beyond bolstering the economy, marine resources are essential for ensuring the food security of countries in the region. Specifically, fish has long been important to approximately 190 million people residing in the coastal areas of the South China Sea. More than 70 per cent of them rely on pelagic fishery resources for their daily protein consumption (Li & Amer, 2015). Take the Philippines as an example, fish contributes to almost 40 per cent of the animal protein supply, while in Indonesia, it accounts for over 50 per cent (Gong *et al.*, 2020).

The impacts of China's maritime militia on the food security of ASEAN countries are twofold. On the one hand, Chinese maritime militia are also involved in fishing activities in addition to military activities, which potentially affect the availability of fishing resources. In fact, China alone makes up 20 per cent of the world's annual fish catch (Harrington, 2022). Alarmingly, more than 95 per cent of the total fish resources in the South China Sea have already been harvested since the 1950s (Gnanasagaran, 2018). If continued, the activities of Chinese militia vessels can contribute to and lead to the depletion of fish stocks in the region.

On the other hand, China's maritime militia also interferes with the freedom of navigation and fishing rights of vessels from other countries. It is believed that the law enforcement vessels and maritime militia of China intimidate and force many Southeast Asian fishermen out of their traditional fishing grounds (Nguyen, 2020). Moreover, since 1999, China has implemented a fishing ban policy in the South China Sea, in effect from May to August. Coupled with this ban, Chinese vessels frequently harass, attack, and sink fishing vessels of other countries, which affects their ability to catch fish and other marine resources (Nguyen, 2020). The actions of the Chinese militia might directly threaten the food security of these ASEAN countries. Other claimant states, such as the Philippines and Vietnam, have publicly opposed China's annual fishing moratorium (Strangio, 2024).

Impacts on the Territorial Security of ASEAN Countries

Together with other maritime forces, the maritime militia of China has conducted a wide range of grey zone activities, such as shadowing, swarming (vessels loitering in large numbers in strategic areas), using military-grade lasers and water cannons against foreign vessels, and many other dangerous manoeuvres (Misalucha-Willoughby, 2023). The presence and activities of Chinese militia vessels in the disputed South China Sea have posed a threat to the territorial integrity of ASEAN countries and regional security, prompting several countries to voice their concerns.

Specifically, the Philippines has many times accused China's maritime militia and the CCG of blocking and harassing its vessels. For example, in June 2019, a Chinese vessel deliberately rammed and sank a Philippine fishing boat in the Recto Bank. All the Filipino fishermen on board were abandoned in the open water ('China Fishing Group Apologises for Philippine Boat Sinking in South China Sea,' 2019). Most recently, in July 2023, the Armed Forces of the Philippines reported that a swarm of 48 Chinese fishing vessels loitered at the Iroquois Reef, near Reed Bank without engaging in fishing activities (Benecki, 2023).

Another notable case is the Haiyang Shiyou 981 standoff between China and Vietnam. On May 2, 2014, the China National Offshore Oil Corporation moved its Haiyang Shiyou 981 oil rig to around 130-150 nautical miles off the Vietnamese coast with the purpose of conducting exploratory drilling ('Letter Dated 3 July 2014 from the Permanent Representative of Viet Nam to the United Nations Addressed to the Secretary-General,' 2014). Vietnam sent its Coast Guard and Fisheries Resources Surveillance forces to disrupt the drilling activities. However, the Vietnamese forces faced strong resistance from a mixed force of PLAN, CCG, and militia vessels (Poling *et al.*, 2021). This incident triggered the highest tension between the two countries. Apart from the Philippines and Vietnam, Malaysia has also condemned the activities of China's maritime militia. The CCG and militia vessels are believed to harass Malaysian oil and gas vessels on a regular basis (Chew, 2021).

In response, Vietnam established its maritime militia with the primary purposes of self-defence and countering China's assertive actions in the South China Sea (Nguyen, 2022). The existence of Vietnam's maritime militia force was first acknowledged in its 2009 'Law on Militia and Self-Defense Forces' (Nguyen, 2022). While the Vietnamese maritime militia is equipped with light weapons (Onishi, 2021), it is still limited in size and capabilities. For a larger and better-equipped Chinese counterpart, Vietnam's militia force is no match (Nguyen & Ton, 2019). Meanwhile, the Philippines is also considering the deployment of its own maritime militia with the aims of bolstering its presence in the West Philippine Sea, safeguarding its sovereignty, and enhancing its patrol capabilities (Elemia, 2023).

In conclusion, the activities of China's maritime militia have infringed upon the sovereignty of ASEAN countries, jeopardising the security and stability of the region. As a consequence, a climate of distrust and uncertainty has emerged among countries. Various Southeast Asian countries have been striving to strengthen their maritime capabilities to tackle China's aggression in the South China Sea.

References

Alien, G. R., Amaoka, K., Anderson Jr, W. D., Bellwood, D. R., Bohlke, E. B., Bradbury, M. G., Carpenter, K. E., Caruso, J. H., Cohen, A. C., & Cohen, D. M. (2000). A checklist of the fishes of the South China Sea. *The Raffles Bulletin of Zoology*, 8, 569–667.

Baijie, A. (2013, April 11). President pays visit to Hainan fishermen. *China Daily*. https://usa.chinadaily.com.cn/2013-04/11/content_16394643.htm

Benecki, P. (2023, July 10). 'Swarm' of Chinese Vessels Spotted Near Strategic Reed Bank. *The Maritime Executive*. https://maritime-executive.com/article/swarm-of-chinese-vessels-spotted-near-strategic-reed-bank

Campbell, C., & Salidjanova, N. (2016). *South China Sea Arbitration Ruling: What Happened and What's Next*? U.S.-China Economic and Security Review Commission. https://www.uscc.gov/research/south-china-sea-arbitration-ruling-what-happened-and-whats-next

Chew, A. (2021, October 25). China harassing Malaysian oil and gas vessels on 'daily' basis: US think tank. *South China Morning Post*. https://www.scmp.com/week-asia/

politics/article/3153648/china-harassing-malaysian-oil-and-gas-vessels-daily-basis-asia

China Fishing Group Apologises for Philippine boat sinking in South China Sea. (2019, August 29). *The Straits Times.* https://www.straitstimes.com/asia/se-asia/china-fishing-group-apologises-for-philippine-boat-sinking-in-south-china-sea

Damayanti, I. (2024, May 30). ASEAN chief says South China Sea code to be concluded by 2025. *Nikkei Asia.* https://asia.nikkei.com/Editor-s-Picks/Interview/ASEAN-chief-says-South-China-Sea-code-to-be-concluded-by-2025

Elemia, C. (2023, August 10). Military chief: Philippines to deploy maritime militia in South China Sea. *Benar News.* https://www.benarnews.org/english/news/philippine/maritime-militia-08102023135600.html

Erickson, A. S. (2017, September 8). Understanding China's Third Sea Force: The Maritime Militia. *Fairbank Center for Chinese Studies.* https://fairbank.fas.harvard.edu/research/blog/understanding-chinas-third-sea-force-the-maritime-militia/

Erickson, A. S., & Kennedy, C. (2015, September 11). Directing China's "Little Blue Men": Uncovering the Maritime Militia Command Structure. *Asia Maritime Transparency Initiative.* https://amti.csis.org/directing-chinas-little-blue-men-uncovering-the-maritime-militia-command-structure/

Erickson, A. S., & Kennedy, C. M. (2016). China's Maritime Militia. In *Becoming a Great 'Maritime Power': A Chinese Dream* (pp. 62–83). Center for Naval Analyses (CNA).

Geraci, M. (2019, June 14). The South China Sea Maritime Tracker. *Institute for China-America Studies.* https://chinaus-icas.org/research/the-south-china-sea-maritime-tracker/

Gnanasagaran, A. (2018, July 22). *Fishy business in the South China Sea.* The ASEAN Post. https://theaseanpost.com/article/fishy-business-south-china-sea

Gong, L., Trajano, J. C. I., Sembiring, M., & Astuti, R. (2020). Marine Environment Protection in the South China Sea. In *Non-Traditional Security Issues in ASEAN: Agendas for Action* (pp. 94–138). ISEAS – Yusof Ishak Institute.

Hale, E. (2021, November 19). China uses maritime militia to assert claim on South China Sea. *Al Jazeera.* https://www.aljazeera.com/news/2021/11/19/china-supports-maritime-militia-to-assert-south-china-sea-claim

Harrington, K. (2022, February 5). South China Sea may run out of fish at this rate of overfishing. *Channel NewsAsia.* https://www.channelnewsasia.com/commentary/south-china-sea-china-environmental-ecological-damage-coral-reefs-overfishing-international-law-2469871

Hayton, B. (2014). *The South China Sea: The Struggle for Power in Asia.* Yale University Press.

Hu, B. (2022). *China's Maritime Militia in the South China Sea: Myths and Realities* (IP22032). Institute of Defence and Strategic Studies. https://www.rsis.edu.sg/rsis-publication/idss/ip22032-chinas-maritime-militia-in-the-south-china-sea-myths-and-realities/

Huang, A.-H., & Hung, M.-T. (2021). 中共海上民兵執行南海「灰色地帶」行動之研究 [A Study on the Chinese Maritime Militia's 'Gray Zone' Operations in the South China Sea]. 國防雜誌 [*National Defense Journal*], 36(1), 23–48. https://doi.org/10.6326/NDJ.202103_36(1).0002

Hui, Z., & Michael, W. (2017). South China Sea: Its Importance for Shipping, Trade, Energy and Fisheries. *Asia-Pacific Journal of Ocean Law and Policy*, 2(1), 9–24. https://doi.org/10.1163/24519391-00201003

Kraska, J., & Monti, M. (2015). The Law of Naval Warfare and China's Maritime Militia. *International Law Studies*, 91. https://digital-commons.usnwc.edu/ils/vol91/iss1/13/

Kuok, L. (2019). *How China's actions in the South China Sea undermine the rule of law*. Brookings. https://www.brookings.edu/articles/how-chinas-actions-in-the-south-china-sea-undermine-the-rule-of-law/

Lalremsiami, C., & Patnaik, J. K. (2020). India in the South China Sea: Role and Implications. *Mizuram University Journal of Humanities and Social Sciences*, *VI*(2), 127–136.

Law of the People's Republic of China on National Defence. (1997). *Database of Laws and Regulations*. http://www.npc.gov.cn/zgrdw/englishnpc/Law/2007-12/11/content_1383547.htm#

Letter dated 3 July 2014 from the Permanent Representative of Viet Nam to the United Nations addressed to the Secretary-General. (2014). *United Nations*. https://digitallibrary.un.org/record/775145

Li, J., & Amer, R. (2015). Closing the Net Against IUU Fishing in the South China Sea: China's Practice and Way Forward. *Journal of International Wildlife Law & Policy*, 18(2), 139–164. https://doi.org/10.1080/13880292.2015.1044799

Luo, S., & Panter, J. G. (2021). China's Maritime Militia and Fishing Fleets: A Primer for Operational Staffs and Tactical Leaders. *Military Review*, 7–21. https://www.armyupress.army.mil/Journals/Military-Review/English-Edition-Archives/January-February-2021/Panter-Maritime-Militia/

McDevitt, M. (2016). *Becoming a Great "Maritime Power": A Chinese Dream*. Center for Naval Analyses. https://www.cna.org/reports/2016/china-becoming-a-maritime-power

McLaughlin, R. (2022, April 6). The Law of the Sea and Grey Zone Operations in the South China Sea. *Institute of Defence and Strategic Studies*. https://www.rsis.edu.sg/rsis-publication/idss/ip22025-the-law-of-the-sea-and-grey-zone-operations-in-the-south-china-sea/

Military Service Law of the People's Republic of China. (1984). *Asian Legal Information Institute*. http://www.asianlii.org/cn/legis/cen/laws/mslotproc463/

Misalucha-Willoughby, C. (2023, November 1). *Let's Call China's Actions in the South China Sea What They Really Are.* United States Institute of Peace. https://www.usip.org/publications/2023/11/lets-call-chinas-actions-south-china-sea-what-they-really-are

Miura, K. (2021). *The Domestic Sources of China's Maritime Assertiveness Under Xi Jinping.* Wilson Center. https://www.wilsoncenter.org/publication/domestic-sources-chinas-maritime-assertiveness-under-xi-jinping

Nguyen, C. V. H. (2020, September 21). Vietnam's Struggles in the South China Sea: Challenges and Opportunities. *Center for International Maritime Security.* https://cimsec.org/vietnams-struggles-in-the-south-china-sea-challenges-and-opportunities/

Nguyen, H. T., & Ton, N. T. B. (2019). Maritime Militias in the South China Sea. *The National Bureau of Asian Research.* https://map.nbr.org/2019/06/maritime-militias-in-the-south-china-sea/

Nguyen, K. G. (2022). *The Vietnamese Maritime Militia: Myths and Realities* (IP22040). https://www.rsis.edu.sg/rsis-publication/idss/ip22040-the-vietnamese-maritime-militia-myths-and-realities/

Onishi, T. (2021, June 12). Vietnam expands maritime militia off southern coast. *Nikkei Asia.* https://asia.nikkei.com/Politics/International-relations/South-China-Sea/Vietnam-expands-maritime-militia-off-southern-coast

Poling, G. B. (2022a). Interests That Abide. In *On Dangerous Ground: America's Century in the South China Sea.* Oxford University Press. https://doi.org/10.1093/oso/9780197633984.003.0001

Poling, G. B. (2022b, January 29). Beijing's self-sabotage in the South China Sea. *East Asia Forum.* https://www.eastasiaforum.org/2022/01/29/beijings-self-sabotage-in-the-south-china-sea/

Poling, G. B., Mallory, T. G., & Prétat, H. (2021). Pulling Back the Curtain on China's Maritime Militia. *Center for Strategic and International Studies.*

Sacks, B. J. (2022). The Political Geography of the South China Sea Disputes. *RAND Corporation.* https://doi.org/10.7249/PEA2021-1

Schofield, C. (2016). Untangling a Complex Web: Understanding Competing Maritime Claims in the South China Sea. In *The South China Sea Dispute: Navigating Diplomatic and Strategic Tensions* (pp. 21–46). ISEAS – Yusof Ishak Institute. https://doi.org/10.1355/9789814695565-003

Steeds, C. (2022). Why have the People's Republic of China and the Socialist Republic of Vietnam been able to create and sustain maritime militias? *Contemporary Voices: The St Andrews Journal of International Relations,* 4(1). https://doi.org/10.15664/jtr.1557

Strangio, S. (2024, May 29). Philippines Vows to Protect Filipino Fishermen Amid Chinese Fishing Ban. *The Diplomat.* https://thediplomat.com/2024/05/philippines-vows-to-protect-filipino-fishermen-amid-chinese-fishing-ban

Strating, B. (2022, April 12). China's nine-dash line proves stranger than fiction. *Lowy Institute*. https://www.lowyinstitute.org/the-interpreter/china-s-nine-dash-line-proves-stranger-fiction

The Ebb and Flow of Beijing's South China Sea Militia. (2022, November 9). *Asia Maritime Transparency Initiative*. https://amti.csis.org/the-ebb-and-flow-of-beijings-south-china-sea-militia/

Yatsuzuka, M. (2023, January 16). How China's maritime militia takes advantage of the grey zone. *The Strategist*. https://www.aspistrategist.org.au/how-chinas-maritime-militia-takes-advantage-of-the-grey-zone/

Yoo, S. J., & Koo, M. G. (2022). Is China Responsible for Its Maritime Militia's Internationally Wrongful Acts? The Attribution of the Conduct of a Parastatal Entity to the State. *Business and Politics*, 24(3), 277–291.

Zhang, H., & Bateman, S. (2017). Fishing Militia, the Securitization of Fishery and the South China Sea Dispute. *Contemporary Southeast Asia*, 39(2), 288–314. http://www.jstor.org/stable/44683771

4

The US FONOP Exercises & China's Submarine Patrols in the South China Sea Region: Challenges to ASEAN States' EEZ Rights

Jeslyn Tan

Abstract

Over the past few years, the situation in the South China Sea has evolved from being a critical sea lane of communication with overlapping maritime boundaries and territorial claims to becoming a theatre for the strategic rivalry between the United States (US) and China, especially for their arms race. China's nuclear ballistic missile submarines (SSBNs) are now conducting 'near-constant' patrols in the South China Sea. The SSBN patrols constitute a part of China's bigger strategy to acquire full control of the contested waters through monitoring and surveillance. On the other hand, the US has increased its military presence in the South China Sea significantly through military operations with its allies and partners as well as the Freedom of Navigation Operations (FONOPs). The FONOPs aim at countering China's excessive maritime claims in the South China Sea; nonetheless, some Southeast Asian countries have reservations about the US FONOPs due to the different interpretations of the 1982 United Nations Convention on the Law of the Sea (UNCLOS). This paper seeks to examine the US FONOPs and China's submarine patrols in the South China Sea and then analyses their challenges to ASEAN states' sovereign rights and jurisdictions in their Exclusive Economic Zones (EEZs) in the contested waters.

Key Words: US FONOP, China, UNCLOS, Submarine Patrols, EEZ rights, South China Sea.

Introduction

The South China Sea is a critical sea lane of communication for connectivity, global maritime trade, and energy supply. It is estimated that Asia accounts for 60 per cent of the global seaborne trade, and one-third of global shipping passes through the South China Sea (*China Power*, 2023). The South China Sea is also crucial for the energy security of regional states, particularly China, Japan, and South Korea as it connects these Northeast Asian states with oil and gas-producing states in the Indian Ocean and Oceania. Furthermore, the South China Sea consists of rich marine resources like hydrocarbon reserves, fish stocks, and rare-earth elements, which are indispensable for the economic development of coastal states.

Nonetheless, over the recent years, the security landscape in the South China Sea has experienced tremendous changes. The important sea lane has become a bone of contention between the coastal states with overlapping maritime territorial and boundary claims, including China, Brunei, Malaysia, the Philippines, and Vietnam. China has become more assertive and aggressive in advancing its historic 'nine-dash line' claims in the South China Sea through 'grey-zone' tactics by using the China Coast Guard (CCG) and the maritime militias to obstruct the operations of other Southeast Asian claimants in the disputed waters.

The escalating altercations between the Philippines and China are worrying. The Philippines' resupply missions to its outposts in the South China Sea, notably to the BRP Sierra Madre in Second Thomas Shoal have been repeatedly harassed by the CCG with water cannons and military-grade lasers, which menaced the safety and security of the Filipino crew (The Associated Press, 2023). The CCG vessels also attempted dangerous manoeuvres in the South China Sea by coming very close to the Philippine vessels, which caused safety of navigation concerns and led to a collision (Wright, 2023). Besides, CCG and the Chinese maritime militias maintain a near-constant presence in Malaysia's Exclusive Economic Zones (EEZs) in Luconia Shoal, obstructing its oil and gas explorations (Asia Maritime Transparency Initiative (AMTI), 2023). In addition to the visible surface vessels, Chinese submarines are said to be conducting "near-continuous" patrols in the South China Sea, including with its nuclear ballistic missile submarines (SSBNs) (US Department of Defence 2023a, p. 108).

Apart from China's increasingly aggressive manoeuvres, another significant development in the South China Sea is the "internationalisation" of the territorial disputes as the contested waters have become the theatre for major power rivalry. Countries like the United States (US), Japan, Australia, India, South Korea, the European Union (EU) (France, Germany, and the Netherlands), Canada, and the United Kingdom (UK) have released their Indo-Pacific strategies and increased their military activities and Freedom of Navigation Operations (FONOPs) in the South China Sea. The US, in particular, has become more proactive in conducting FONOPs and joint military drills with allies and partners in the South China Sea against the backdrop of intensifying geopolitical competition with China in the region.

Against such background, this paper aims to suggest that both the US FONOPs and China's submarine patrols pose challenges to the sovereign rights and jurisdictions of the Association of Southeast Asian Nations (ASEAN) states in their EEZs in the South China Sea. This paper will first examine the US FONOPs and China's submarine patrols in the South China Sea and then analyse the challenges that these activities bring towards ASEAN states' sovereign rights and jurisdictions in the disputed waters.

US FONOPS in the South China Sea

In the South China Sea, the US has upped its military operations—a move that irritates China as Beijing believes it has sovereign control over the South China Sea. Washington has been conducting FONOPs in the disputed waters in an effort to uphold the regional rules-based order and refute China's maritime claims, which it considers to be unlawful under the 1982 United Nations Convention on the Law of the Sea (UNCLOS). The FONOPs began in 1979 to contest the unilateral maritime claims asserted by coastal states, which the US deemed excessive and restrictive to the rights and freedom of navigation and overflight of the international community (USDOD, 2015).

As shown in Figure 4.1, the US FONOPs in the South China Sea from 2018 to 2023 peaked in 2020 with nine FONOPs conducted that year under President Donald Trump's administration. Since President Joe Biden took office in January 2021, the US FONOPs have decreased to an average of five operations per year. In 2023, there were five FONOPs implemented by the US 7th Fleet in the South China Sea, with the latest taking place on December 4 when the USS Gabrielle Giffords sailed through the Second Thomas Shoal. The People's Liberation Army's (PLA) Southern Theatre Command released a statement in response to this, claiming that the littoral combat ship encroached into Chinese waters off Renai Reef (Second Thomas Shoal) in China's Nansha Islands (Spratly Islands) without Beijing's approval and seriously violated Chinese sovereignty as well as the international law (Southern Theatre Command, 2023).

Figure 4.1: US FONOPs in the South China Sea (2018–2023)

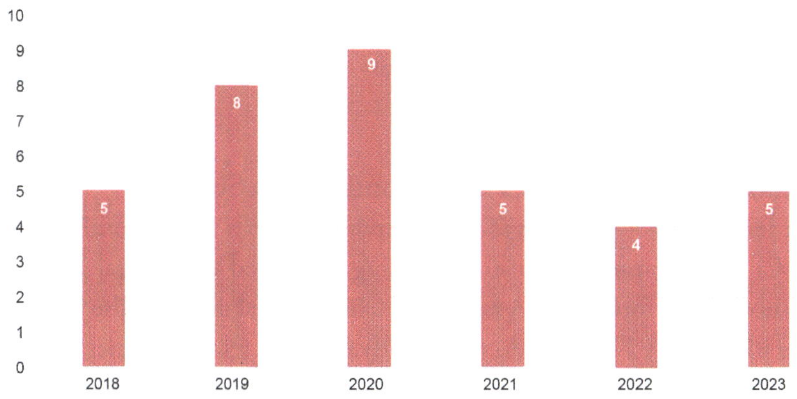

Source: Official Website of the US 7th Fleet (United States 7th Fleet, 2023).

Although the FONOPs implemented by the US have decreased, nonetheless, according to the Beijing-based South China Sea Strategic Situation Probing Initiative (SCSPI), US military activities together with its allies and security partners in the South China Sea have become more politicised and high-profile over the past two years with the language of its statements more critical towards China (South China Sea Strategic Situation Probing Initiative [SCSPI], 2023). This is part of the information warfare against China in order to deter and challenge China's claims in the South China Sea. The think tank estimates that the scale and number of the US military exercises in the South China Sea and surrounding waters have escalated, increasing from 95 in 2021 to 102 in 2022 (SCSPI, 2022 & 2023). Many of them were bilateral or multilateral drills with allies and security partners such as the Association of Southeast Asian Nations (ASEAN) member states, Japan, the UK, Australia, India, France, and Canada.

Among the ASEAN members, the Philippines is the most supportive of the US military activities in the South China Sea and has hosted various large-scale multilateral and bilateral maritime drills with the US and other Indo-Pacific partners in 2023 such as the Maritime Training Activity (MTA) Sama Sama and Exercise Balikatan. As a result of its increased high-profile strategic involvement in the South China Sea, China has long regarded the US as the main peace disruptor in the contested waters. FONOPs in the South China Sea are of paramount importance to the US to deny China's military access to the second island chain where Guam is located; hence, the US is only expected to increase its military presence in the disputed waters in the years to come.

China's Submarine Patrols in the South China Sea

In order to protect its strategic and sovereign interests in the South China Sea, China is committed to strengthening its littoral warfare capabilities. The submarines form an integral part of China's naval defence. The People's Liberation Army Navy (PLAN) currently operates 59 submarines (Dahm & Zhao, 2023, p. 2), and the submarine fleet is expected to increase to 65 units by 2025 and 80 units by 2035 (USDOD, 2023a, p. 55). Table 1 indicates the number of different types of submarines owned by the PLAN that were still active in service in 2023.

China is forming a nuclear and conventional maritime deterrent force under the navy of the Southern Theatre Command based in Zhanjiang, Guangdong. The Southern Theatre Command covers the sea lanes of communication in Southeast Asia, including monitoring US FONOPs and military activities in the South China Sea, ensures security along the China-Southeast Asia border, as well as provides support to the PLA in case of a Taiwan contingency (USDOD, 2023A, p. 122). Hainan Island, China's closest point to the South China Sea serves as a military garrison for the Southern Theatre Navy with the Yalong Naval Base and the Yulin Naval Basc. Yalong Naval Base is the homeport for all of the six Jin-class SSBNs and two of the Shang-class SSNs, while the Yulin Naval Base docks 11 SS and China's first domestically produced aircraft carrier, Shandong.

Table 4.1: PLAN Submarines Active in 2023

NATO Name	Plan Designator	Number of Active Submarines in 2023
Jin-class SSBN	Type 094, 094A	6
Shang-class nuclear-powered attack submarine (SSN)	Type 093, 093A/B	6
Yuan-class air-independent propulsion attack submarine (SSP)	Type 039A/B/C/D	20
Song-class diesel-electric powered attack submarine (SS)	Type 039, 039G	13
Qing-class auxiliary submarine (SSA)	Type 032	1
Kilo-class SS	Type 636	10
Ming-class SS	Type 035	3
	Total	**59**

Source: Dahm, J. M. and Zhao, A. (2023). China Maritime Report No. 28: Bitterness Ends, Sweetness Begins: Organizational Changes to the PLAN Submarine Force Since 2015.

The submarines of the PLAN consist of two formations: information support and naval assault (Dahm & Zhao, 2023, p. 13). The information support formation is responsible for intelligence, surveillance, and reconnaissance (ISR) to gather information on targeted rivals, whereas the naval assault formation is responsible for anti-surface warfare (Dahm & Zhao, 2023). A third one might be added in the future on submarine-uncrewed underwater vehicles (UUVs) as China reportedly conducted testing for two extra-large uncrewed underwater vehicles (XLUUVs) on a naval base (could be Yulin or Yalong) in Hainan in 2022 (Dahm & Zhao, 2023; Sutton, 2022).

The PLAN is determined to strengthen its near-seas defence and far-seas protection, notably its sea-based nuclear deterrent amidst Beijing's growing global ambitions and the intensifying geopolitical competition with the US. China's *Jin*-class SSBNs can be equipped with up to 12 JL-2 or JL-3 intercontinental-range submarine-launched ballistic missiles (SLBMs) (USDOD, 2023A, p. 55). A *Jin* SSBN equipped with a 7,200-kilometre range JL-2 SLBMs would have to operate beyond the first island chain to reach the continental US, either in the mid-Pacific Ocean to reach the US West Coast, Hawaii, and Alaska or east of Hawaii to reach the US East Coast (USDOD, 2023A, p. 59; Dahm & Zhao, 2023, p. 18). However, the newer JL-3 SLBMs with a range of over 10,000 kilometres allow the PLAN to target the west coast of the US from Chinese coastal waters (Logan, 2023).

The current Type 094 *Jin*-class SSBNs are a lot noisier than the Russian and US submarines and more easily detected. Therefore, the PLAN has been developing a quieter new-generation Type 096 SSBN which incorporates Russian technology and design and will be harder to detect in the future. This leads to concern about the increasing surveillance network of submarines in the South China Sea which is not easily detectable. According to the Pentagon, the PLAN is able to maintain a constant nuclear deterrence presence in the South China Sea with its six operational Type 094 *Jin*-class SSBNs (USDOD, 2023A, p. 59). However, the location of the Chinese submarines in the disputed waters and the time period of their presence in those waters are ambiguous.

The military outposts on Chinese-made artificial islands in the South China Sea help support the operations of the submarines, CCG, and maritime militias to target the US FONOPs as well as gather intelligence in the EEZs of other claimant states. The PLAN now also has a stronger second-strike capability from a bastion near mainland China with the development of the latest JL-3 SLBMs and Type 096 SSBNs. Furthermore, despite the lack of indication of China's intention to use its SSBNs as deterrence against India, the *Jin*-class SSBNs have the capacity to strike India from the South China Sea without having to sail into the Indian Ocean (Zhao, 2016). The South China Sea holds strategic importance to China's first island chain strategy, especially to its plan for Taiwan reunification (O'Hanlon & Andrew Yeo,

2023). Hence, China will only become more assertive in the South China Sea to prevent a blockade in the maritime area by the US and its allies and the undermining of Beijing's position on Taiwan (O'Hanlon & Andrew Yeo, 2023, p. 2).

Challenges of US FONOPS & China's Submarine Patrols to ASEAN States' EEZ Rights

The US FONOPs, although has been mostly labelled as a challenge against China's illegal and excessive maritime claims in the South China Sea, are in fact also directed at the "excessive" maritime claims of other claimant states like Malaysia, Taiwan, and Vietnam, as pointed out in the 2022 Annual Freedom of Navigation Report released by the US Department of Defense (USDOD, 2023b). Therefore, there are mixed receptions and reactions among ASEAN claimants towards the US FONOPs in the South China Sea (Bateman, 2017 & 2018). Cambodia, Indonesia, Malaysia, the Philippines, Thailand and Vietnam have all set restrictions on the freedoms of navigation by non-littoral states in their jurisdictional waters "not unlike those imposed by China" (Bateman, 2018). For example, Vietnam requires prior notification for foreign warships entering its territorial sea (USDOD, 2023b).

There is a significant difference in the interpretation of freedom of navigation in the EEZs by major powers and littoral states (S. Rajaratnam School of International Studies [RSIS] Maritime Security Program, 2017). Naval powers like the US view "the EEZs [as] an extension inwards of the high seas;" hence, the high seas regime applies in the EEZs. Nonetheless, the littoral states view the EEZs as "an extension outwards of their territorial sea," thus, the freedom of navigation in the EEZs is not absolute (Bateman, 2017).

In the case of Malaysia, Kuala Lumpur prohibits any foreign state from conducting military activities in its EEZs without consent and requests prior notification for nuclear-powered vessels to enter its territorial sea on account of a declaration deposited by the Malaysian Government with the UN Secretary-General on 14 October 1996 upon ratification of UNCLOS (UN Treaty Collection, 1996; Hamzah, 2017). Malaysia understands that there are no provisions under UNCLOS that specifically confer the right to foreign states to conduct military exercises or manoeuvres in EEZs of the littoral states (Hamzah, 2013; RSIS Maritime Security Program, 2017).

Furthermore, from Malaysia's perspective, unauthorised foreign military activities in its EEZs are against the principle of peaceful uses of the sea in UNCLOS (Hamzah, 2013). This is because "activities that are military in nature or result in the production of data to serve military needs" can be used against Malaysia's interests and undermine its territorial integrity and security (RSIS Maritime Security Program, 2017, p. 11), Military activities for instance; include, intelligence collection and surveillance, launching an aircraft, and test-firing weapons. Besides, foreign states that conduct oceanographic research in a coastal state's EEZs may violate the coastal state's jurisdiction over marine scientific research in its EEZs, as stated in Article 56 of UNCLOS (UNCLOS, 1982). Therefore, due to the varying interpretations of UNCLOS, some ASEAN coastal states might perceive that the US FONOPs violate their sovereign integrity and jurisdictions in their maritime areas.

Similarly, China's near-continuous submarine patrols in the South China Sea constitute the same or even greater threat to ASEAN states' sovereign integrity and EEZ rights. This is because the Chinese submarines, including the nuclear-powered submarines, could be in ASEAN states' EEZs constantly, conducting activities that are against the peaceful uses of the sea such as intelligence-gathering, surveillance, or military surveys. The information collected might be used against the interests of the ASEAN claimant states and become detrimental to their national security and sovereignty, particularly in the contested South China Sea.

According to Article 58(1) of the UNCLOS, all ships, including submarines enjoy freedom of navigation in the EEZs of a coastal state like in the high seas and submarines can remain submerged too when passing through the EEZs of a coastal state (UNCLOS, 1982). Nevertheless, there is a grey area in UNCLOS on whether or not intelligence collection during freedom of navigation should be considered "for peaceful purposes" as stated in Article 88, which also applies in the EEZs under Article 58(2) since the information acquired could be prejudicial to the security of the coastal state if related to national defence (UNCLOS, 1982). Moreover, if the Chinese submarines conduct marine scientific research on natural resources in an ASEAN coastal state's EEZs, it may constitute a violation of the ASEAN coastal state's jurisdiction over marine scientific research as well as its sovereign rights to manage and exploit the natural resources in its EEZ (UNCLOS, 1982).

Due to the fact that the submarines operate submerged beneath the sea, it could pose difficulty for the ASEAN states to track and monitor them. China, which deems the South China Sea its internal waters, territorial seas, and the EEZs within the 'nine-dash line' also never gives prior notification and obtains authorisation to operate its submarines in the claimed EEZs of the ASEAN states. Besides, the CCG and Chinese maritime militias' surface vessels have become increasingly assertive and aggressive towards the activities of ASEAN claimants in the South China Sea.

On the other hand, the US FONOPs and China's submarine patrols in the South China Sea also heighten the arms race in the region, particularly with their increased use of nuclear-powered or nuclear-armed submarines and underwater vehicles. Regional states like Malaysia and Indonesia have expressed concerns about the operations of SSNs in their waters with Australia acquiring nuclear submarines from its AUKUS submarine deal. The Southeast Asian nations are concerned that these new developments may potentially induce arms racing and escalate tensions in the region (Ministry of Foreign Affairs of Malaysia, 2023; Ministry of Foreign Affairs of Indonesia, 2021; The White House, 2023). The increasing military activities in the South China Sea could lead to an armed conflict between the US and China in the vital sea lane, a scenario that the ASEAN states seek to prevent as it will have profound implications for the region.

Conclusion

As the military activities of the major powers grow in the South China Sea, challenges to the ASEAN states have also become greater. Due to the different interpretations of UNCLOS, the US FONOPs may infringe on the sovereign rights and jurisdictions of ASEAN claimant states in the South China Sea. However, in general, ASEAN claimants are not entirely against FONOPs as it is a matter of different interpretations of UNCLOS between coastal states and naval powers in terms of 'freedom' or 'right' of navigation. 'Right of navigation,' which has a more restrictive meaning than 'freedom of navigation' is applied to innocent passage in territorial seas and archipelagic waters, whereas 'freedom of navigation' applies to navigation in straits (used for international navigation) and navigation in high seas (Bateman, 2017). Furthermore, the US also acts as a balancer against China in the South China Sea. Most importantly, there are no sovereignty disputes between the US and ASEAN states. Despite ASEAN states being concerned about the looming arms race in the wake of elevated US FONOPs and military activities in the South China Sea, they actively participate in the US-led joint naval exercises and other military engagements.

In comparison to the US, China's near to constant presence in the South China Sea concerns ASEAN claimants more due to the overlapping maritime claims in the South China Sea. CCG and the Chinese maritime militias are constantly obstructing the economic and strategic activities of ASEAN claimants in the contested waters with increased aggression and assertiveness. Furthermore, China's submarines, including SSBNs, are constantly patrolling the South China Sea, with some patrols potentially violating ASEAN coastal states' jurisdictions and sovereign rights. These violations may involve oceanographic research for oil, gas, and other marine resources, which could be seen as infringing on ASEAN states' rights in their EEZs.

Against such a backdrop, ASEAN states can further enhance their defence capability to prevent the incursions of foreign vessels into their maritime areas. Middle powers like Japan, the EU, and India may be able to fill the gap by providing aid to ASEAN states through equipment transfers and capacity-building, for instance, Malaysia and the Philippines were the first batch of recipients of Japan's Official Security Assistance (OSA) worth 2 billion yen (USD 13.5 million) in fiscal year 2023, receiving maritime surveillance equipment including coastal surveillance radars, drones, and fast interceptor boats (Kyodo News, 2023). Indonesia and Vietnam are expected to become recipients of the second batch of the OSA worth about 5 billion yen (USD 33.8 million) in fiscal year 2024, receiving not only satellite communication systems and maritime surveillance systems but also "other forms of aid, such as building ports for military-civilian use, free of charge" (Takahashi, 2023). Such assistance can be very beneficial to improve ASEAN states' maritime defence capability as well as ASEAN-middle power maritime cooperation.

Additionally, middle powers can also provide arms to ASEAN states to strengthen their maritime defence capabilities. In April 2024, India delivered the first batch of BrahMos supersonic cruise missiles to the Philippines. This delivery was part of a USD 375 million deal signed in January 2022, which included three batteries of anti-ship missiles and technical support for the Philippine Marine Corps Coastal Defense Regiment. Manila is now constructing its first BrahMos missile base in Western Luzon, strategically located to face the South China Sea (Lariosa, 2024).

Besides, Malaysia is negotiating with South Korea for an additional 18 units of the FA-50M light combat aircraft, on top of the 18 units it had already purchased from Seoul in May 2023 (Bernama, 2024). The increased defence industrial cooperation between middle powers and ASEAN states indicates their growing role in the military modernisation of ASEAN. By providing affordable yet high-quality military equipment, these collaborations can help bridge the gap in ASEAN's coastal defence capabilities as part of their modernisation efforts.

References

Asia Maritime Transparency Initiative (AMTI). (2023). *Flooding the Zone: China Coast Guard Patrols in 2022.* Center for Strategic and International Studies (CSIS). https://amti.csis.org/flooding-the-zone-china-coast-guard-patrols-in-2022/

Bateman, S. (2017). *Freedom of navigation is in the eye of the beholder*, East Asia Forum, https://eastasiaforum.org/2017/08/24/freedom-of-navigation-is-in-the-eye-of-the-beholder/

Bateman, S. (2018). *No need to rock the boat in the South China Sea*, East Asia Forum, https://eastasiaforum.org/2018/03/06/no-need-to-rock-the-boat-in-the-south-china-sea/

Bernama. (2024). *Malaysia 'Very Much Likely' to Order Additional 18 Units of FA-50M – KAI Official*, https://www.bernama.com/en/news.php?id=2294910

ChinaPower. (2023). *How Is China's Energy Footprint Changing?* Center for Strategic and International Studies (CSIS). https://chinapower.csis.org/energy-footprint/.

Dahm, J. M. & Zhao, A. (2023). China Maritime Report No. 28: Bitterness Ends, Sweetness Begins: Organizational Changes to the PLAN Submarine Force Since 2015. *CMSI China Maritime Reports*. https://digital-commons.usnwc.edu/cmsi-maritime-reports/28

Hamzah, B. A. (2013). Foreign military activities in the EEZ: preliminary views from Malaysia, in *Securing the Safety of Navigation in East Asia: Legal and Political Dimensions*, (ed.) by Shicun Wu and Keyuan Zou, Oxford, Cambridge, Philadelphia, and New Delhi: Chandos Publishing, pp. 161-169.

Hamzah, B. A. (2017). Unauthorised Manoeuvres in Waters: US Chides Msia Restrictions, *RSIS Commentary*. Vol. 88.

Kyodo News. (2023). *Japan to provide rescue boats to Malaysian military amid China's rise*. https://english.kyodonews.net/news/2024/02/33b5e4b96c1f-urgent-classified-japanese-diplomatic-info-leaked-after-chinese-cyberattacks.html

Lariosa, A. (2024). Philippines Builds First BrahMos Anti-Ship Missile Base Facing South China Sea, *Naval News*. https://www.navalnews.com/naval-news/2024/06/philippines-builds-first-brahmos-anti-ship-missile-base-facing-south-china-sea/

Logan, D. C. (2023). China Maritime Report No. 33: China's Sea-Based Nuclear Deterrent: Organizational, Operational, and Strategic Implications. *CMSI China Maritime Reports*. https://digital-commons.usnwc.edu/cgi/viewcontent.cgi?article=1032&context=cmsi-maritime-reports

Ministry of Foreign Affairs of Indonesia. (2021). *Statement on Australia's Nuclear-powered Submarines Program*, https://kemlu.go.id/portal/en/read/2937/siaran_pers/statement-on-australias-nuclear-powered-submarines-program

Ministry of Foreign Affairs of Malaysia. (2023). *Enhanced Trilateral Security Partnership Between Australia, the United Kingdom and the United States of America (AUKUS)*, https://www.kln.gov.my/web/guest/-/enhanced-trilateral-security-partnership-between-australia-the-united-kingdom-and-the-united-states-of-america-aukus-

O'Hanlon, M. E. & Yeo, A. (2023). *Geostrategic competition and overseas basing in East Asia and the First Island Chain*, The Brookings Institution, https://www.brookings.edu/articles/geostrategic-competition-and-overseas-basing-in-east-asia-and-the-first-island-chain/

S. Rajaratnam School of International Studies (RSIS) Maritime Security Program. (2017). *Understanding Freedoms of Navigation—ASEAN Perspectives*, https://www.rsis.edu.sg/wp-content/uploads/2017/08/ER170808_Freedom-of-Navigation_WEB.pdf

South China Sea Strategic Situation Probing Initiative (SCSPI). (2022). *An Incomplete Report on US Military Activities in the South China Sea in 2021*, http://www.scspi.org/sites/default/files/reports/an_incomplete_report_on_us_military_activities_in_the_south_china_sea_in_2021_0.pdf

South China Sea Strategic Situation Probing Initiative (SCSPI). (2023). *An Incomplete Report on US Military Activities in the South China Sea in 2022*, http://www.scspi.org/sites/default/files/reports/an_incomplete_report_on_us_military_activities0ain_the_south_china_sea_in_2022.pdf

Southern Theatre Command. (2023). *nanbu zhanqu xinwenfayanren jiu mei jian shanchuang zhongguo nansha renai jiao linjin haiyu fabiao tanhua* [Statement from the Southern Theatre Command on the US warship's trespassing into waters adjacent to Ren'ai Reef in China's Nansha Islands], http://www.mod.gov.cn/gfbw/qwfb/16270670.html

Sutton, H. I. (2022). Chinas New Extra-Large Submarine Drones Revealed, *Naval News*. https://www.navalnews.com/naval-news/2022/09/chinas-secret-extra-large-submarine-drone-program-revealed/

Takahashi, A. (2023). Japan eyes 6 nations to receive security aid in fiscal 2024, *The Asahi Shimbun*, https://www.asahi.com/ajw/articles/14991342

The Associated Press. (2023). Philippines says the Chinese coast guard attacked its vessels for a second day, *National Public Radio (NPR)*, https://www.npr.org/2023/12/10/1218439284/philippines-says-the-chinese-coast-guard-attacked-its-vessels-for-a-second-day

The White House, (2023). *Fact Sheet: Trilateral Australia-UK-US Partnership on Nuclear-Powered Submarines*, https://www.whitehouse.gov/briefing-room/statements-releases/2023/03/13/fact-sheet-trilateral-australia-uk-us-partnership-on-nuclear-powered-submarines/

UN Treaty Collection. (1996). *Malaysia: Declaration Upon Ratification of UNCLOS*, United Nations, https://treaties.un.org/Pages/ViewDetailsIII.aspx?src=TREATY&mtdsg_no=XXI-6&chapter=21&Temp=mtdsg3&clang=_en#EndDec

United Nations. (1982). *United Nations Convention on the Law of the Sea*. https://www.un.org/depts/los/convention_agreements/texts/unclos/unclos_e.pdf

United States 7th Fleet. (2023). *News from 2018-2023*, https://www.c7f.navy.mil/Media/News/

US Department of Defense (DOD). (2015). *Freedom of Navigation Program: Fact Sheet*, https://policy.defense.gov/Portals/11/Documents/gsa/cwmd/DoD%20FON%20Program%20--%20Fact%20Sheet%20(March%202015).pdf

US Department of Defense (DOD). (2023a). *Military and Security Developments Involving the People's Republic of China*, https://media.defense.gov/2023/Oct/19/2003323409/-1/-1/1/2023-military-and-security-developments-involving-the-peoples-republic-of-china.pdf

US Department of Defense (DOD). (2023b). *Annual Freedom of Navigation Report: Fiscal Year 2022*, https://policy.defense.gov/Portals/11/Documents/FON%20Program%20Report_FY2022.pdf?ver=8of4c3mCAOnzfa4AfTYIyg%3d%3d

Wright, G. (2023). South China Sea: Philippine and Chinese vessels collide in contested waters, *British Broadcasting Corporation (BBC)*. https://www.bbc.com/news/world-asia-67668930

Zhao, T. (2016). *China's Sea-Based Nuclear Deterrent*, Carnegie Endowment for International Peace, https://carnegieendowment.org/2016/06/30/china-s-sea-based-nuclear-deterrent-pub-63909

5

Viet Nam—India Defence and Security Cooperation: Any New Impetus to Bolster?

Nguyen Thi Lan Huong

Abstract

From "bilateral relations" to "strategic partnership," to now a "comprehensive strategic partnership", Viet Nam and India have shared close diplomatic ties and mutual interests. This long-standing relationship comprises 4 pillars: diplomatic-political covering strategic dimensions, economic, defence, and people-to-people. As said Indian External Affairs Minister S. Jaishankar, the comprehensive strategic partnership between India and Viet Nam was emerging as a "source of security, stability and progress in the region." In the context of more fragmented world, we see the dynamic strategic shift to the Indo-Pacific, and increasing grey-zone tactics in the region which blur the line between war and peace. This paper aims to analyse challenges and opportunities and find out ways to intensify bilateral practical cooperation, particularly in the maritime domain.

Key Words: India, Viet Nam, Defence relations, Comprehensive Strategic Partnership, Maritime Domain.

A Brief Overview of Indo-Vietnam Defence Relations

Over the past 52 years, Viet Nam and India have broadened and deepened their bilateral relations, upgraded to a strategic partnership and then to a comprehensive strategic partnership. Both sides share mutual interests and concerns at the bilateral, regional and international levels. Up to now, Viet Nam and India have demonstrated strategic trust and a political commitment to implementing the comprehensive strategic partnership, through high-level visits and practical cooperation in various areas, including in the domain of maritime cooperation.

Given the present circumstances, there is a growing set of strategic dynamics and emerging hybrid challenges, such as the major powers' rivalry or the 'might is right' policy with grey-zone activities which would affect regional peace, stability and prosperity: (i) Chinese coercive behaviour in the Indo-Pacific region seems to be a factor pushing India to have a shift in stance on the South China Sea issue for the first time; (ii) Amidst various perspectives on the Indo-Pacific by different players and stakeholders, India and ASEAN also share common views on the region; in the meanwhile, emerging groupings of countries could raise concern over the ASEAN Centrality.

Recommendations for bolstering cooperation between India and ASEAN, including Viet Nam: (i) India and Viet Nam should keep in the right direction at the bilateral level; (ii) From a broader perspective, India and ASEAN, including Viet Nam could synchronise or synergise the key elements in the IPOI and the AOIP to promote maritime cooperation and maritime connectivity while emphasising the ASEAN Centrality; (iii) Many initiatives by the QUAD could contribute to make transparency in the Indo-Pacific, i.e.: the Indo-Pacific Partnership for Maritime Domain Awareness or the QUAD Partnership for Cable Connectivity and Resilience. India could be a focal point to help ASEAN and QUAD countries to work together in the coming years, including but not limited to the field of MDA or submarine cable security.

Introduction

Over the past 52 years, Viet Nam and India have broadened and deepened their bilateral relations, upgraded to a strategic partnership, and then, to a comprehensive strategic partnership by sharing mutual interests and concerns at the bilateral, regional and international levels. This traditional relationship focuses on four pillars: diplomatic-political covering strategic dimensions, economic, defence, and people-to-people. During Indian External Affairs Minister S. Jaishankar's official working visit in Ha Noi in October 2023, he highlighted that the comprehensive strategic partnership between India and Viet Nam has built on that, emerging as a source of security, stability and progress in the region. Among four pillars of the traditional relationship, including diplomatic-political covering strategic dimensions; economic; people-to-people, defence and security cooperation is a key pillar.

This paper will have an overview on bilateral ties, focusing on defence and security cooperation. By assessing the strategic environment with emerging threats in the Indo-Pacific, this paper will suggest potential ways forward to enhance practical cooperation between Viet Nam and India in the coming years, especially in the maritime domain, contributing to the promotion of the rules-based architecture in the region.

Viet Nam—India: Time-Tested Friendship, Multifaceted Partnership

Viet Nam and India have traditional and long-standing ties, with close links in culture and history. From the establishment of diplomatic relations in January 1972, they upgraded bilateral relations to the strategic partnership in 2007, and then to a comprehensive strategic partnership in September 2016. Built on a firm foundation, both countries share mutual trust and understanding as well as strong mutual support in the international and regional fora. India views Viet Nam as an important pillar in India's Act East Policy. Viet Nam and India cooperate in various fields, including (i) Defence and Security, (ii) Economy, Trade and Investment, (iii) Development, (iv) Scientific and Technological domains, (v) Regional and International mechanisms and (vi) Other areas (Energy, Connectivity, Health, Culture, Tourism and People-to-people relations and training) (Full Joint Statement between Viet Nam-India, 2018). In 2020, the prime ministers of both countries announced a joint vision for peace, prosperity and people to guide the future development of Viet Nam-India comprehensive strategic partnership.

Amongst a range of areas of cooperation, defence and security cooperation is the first pillar of this comprehensive strategic partnership, achieving significant results as outlined below:

Firstly, Viet Nam and India laid the groundwork for fostering greater understanding and collaboration by inking several important documents, including the joint vision statement on Viet Nam-India defence cooperation for the period of 2015-2020, the joint vision statement on Viet Nam-India defence partnership towards 2030, and the memorandum of understanding on mutual logistic support (2022). While India concluded several logistics arrangements with various countries such as France, Oman, the Philippines, Singapore, South Korea and Australia (Pant, 2019), this marks the first time Viet Nam has signed a Memorandum of Understanding of this nature with any nation.

Secondly, the two countries conduct diversified defence collaborations, such as defence security exchanges and dialogues, human resources training and collaboration between the army, air force, naval and coast guard, as well as cooperation in cyber security and information sharing. The first defence line of credit in the amount of USD 100 million was signed and implemented for the building of 12 offshore high-speed patrol boats. Recently, India offered a USD 500 million defence line of credit to the defence industry and USD 5 million in funding for the construction of an army software park at the telecommunication university in Nha Trang (Embassy of India in Hanoi, 2021). India gifted two simulators and a monetary grant towards setting up of Language and IT Lab at the Air Force Officers Training School for capacity building of Vietnamese armed forces, activated a satellite imaging and tracking station in Ha Noi, enabling it to track vessels and ships activities in the region (Miglani, Torode, 2016). In addition, both countries have collaborated in United Nations peacekeeping missions and enhanced coordination within various multilateral defence and security cooperation frameworks such as the ASEAN-led fora, including the ASEAN Regional Forum and the ASEAN Defence Ministers Meeting.

It can be observed that Viet Nam and India have expanded their maritime cooperation through bilateral dialogues, port visits and bilateral exercises. Both sides have held 3 maritime security dialogues since 2019. In 2023, in the third maritime security dialogue in New Delhi, both sides vowed to further strengthen their shared efforts and existing frameworks in areas such as marine scientific research, Humanitarian Assistance and Disaster Relief (HADR), maritime connectivity and maritime security, including navy and coast guard cooperation, maritime law enforcement and capacity building (Khanh Nguyen, 2023). In terms of port calls and visits between the two countries, a Viet Nam coast guard vessel docked at Chennai Port, India for the first time in 2018 (VNA, 2018). Indian coast guard and naval ships have made frequent port calls and visits to Viet Nam, some notable instances include the November 2022 port call to Ho Chi Minh City and the visit to Da Nang port in May 2023 (Embassy of India in Ha Noi, 2023), together with training cooperation program (Minh Vu, 2021). Viet Nam has regularly participated in the MILAN naval exercise hosted by the Indian Navy and joined the Viet Nam-India Bilateral Army Exercise (VINBAX in 2018). In 2023, for the first time, India gifted INS Kirpan, a fully operational, in-service corvette to Viet Nam (Singh, 2023).

Gaining Momentum for Further Cooperation?

So far, there is no denying that Viet Nam and India have demonstrated strategic trust to develop a comprehensive strategic partnership (Peri, 2023), marked by a broader alignment of interests and shared concerns and through practical cooperation. To date, they have observed substantial and significant advancements in defence and security cooperation, particularly in the maritime domain.

The next point of inquiry is whether there is any potential for further promoting this deep-rooted partnership. We should analyse this relationship within a broader strategic context, rather than solely focusing on the bilateral aspect. In the joint vision for peace, prosperity, and people in 2020, the leaders agreed that enhanced defence and security bilateral partnership will be an important factor of stability in the Indo-Pacific region.

Given the present circumstances, there is a growing set of strategic dynamics and emerging challenges, including the major powers' rivalry or the 'might is right' policy, which would affect regional peace and prosperity. Indeed, as coastal states in the Indo-Pacific and parties to the 1982 United

Nations Convention on the Law of the Sea (UNCLOS), Viet Nam and India both share common concerns related to regional maritime security, in maintaining peace, stability, prosperity, freedom and safety of navigation and of overflight and in promoting the rules-based order at sea.

Coercive Actions: Challenge for the Regional Rule-Based Architecture?

In 2023, China issued a new map triggering many countries in the Indo-Pacific, including Viet Nam and India (Ebbighausen, 2023). This is not the first time that China has used maps as a diplomatic and legal tool to assert its territorial and maritime claims. In 2009, China publicly released a nine-dash line map to the United Nations to assert maritime claims in the South China Sea without any clarification. However, this excessive claim faced the international community's protests, and in 2016, the arbitral tribunal in the famous South China Sea Arbitration case rejected the nine-dash line claim in its final ruling. In response, China gradually adopted legal arguments based on the '*Nanhai Zhudao*' (*Four sha*) to defend its territorial claims and maritime rights in the South China Sea. With this claim, China also expresses a larger ambition to transform undisputed maritime zones into disputed ones. China's new formula of the '*Nanhai Zhudao*' position has been opposed by a number of countries, not limited to South China Sea claimants but including various regional stakeholders in the Indo-Pacific, through the diplomatic notes exchanges in the United Nations during the period 2019-2022. In 2023, India has experienced a shift in its stance on the South China Sea issue. In a Joint Statement on June 29, 2023, India and the Philippines "underlined the need for peaceful settlement of disputes and for adherence to international law, especially the UNCLOS and the 2016 arbitral award on the South China Sea in this regard." This marks the first time India has called for parties to abide by the rulings. Previously, in 2016, India had made an official statement noting the award of the case, supporting freedom of navigation and overflight, and peaceful dispute settlement (MEA India, Statement on Award of Arbitral Tribunal on the South China Sea, 2016).

In addition to this active legal warfare, China uses targeted economic coercion many times. India is also concerned about the Chinese Belt and Road and Maritime Silk Road initiatives due to sovereignty issues and economic trade-offs (Sharma, 2022). Moreover, China frequently employs its grey-zone strategy in the region by reinforcing its vessels' presence to expand its footprint in the maritime domain. China skillfully applies the 'cabbage strategy' by deploying a number of vessels (fishing vessels, maritime militia vessels, research vessels), not only in the South China Sea and the East China Sea but also in the Indian Ocean. In a very recent report published in 2024 by the Centre for Strategic and International Studies (CSIS) in Washington DC, it is shown that China is also expanding its surveying operations from its maritime periphery in the South China Sea and the western Pacific Ocean to the Indian Ocean—an "emerging arena of competition between Beijing and New Delhi" (et al., 2024; Hart and Powers-Riggs, 2024). Many international observers raised concern over the presence of Chinese vessels, viewed as an emerging hybrid threat to Indian maritime security (Sakhuja, 2021).

A Maze of Various Ideas under the Umbrella of "Indo-Pacific"

Over the past years, there has been a noticeable strategic shift towards the Indo-Pacific region. This is evident as various stakeholders, both within and outside the region, have their own perspectives on the Indo-Pacific with distinct principles, pillars and priorities due to divergent interests and calculations. Furthermore, there is a growing tendency of 'minilateralism' with new groupings such as QUAD, AUKUS, etc. To some extent, these initiatives or emerging minilateral groupings of like-minded countries are interpreted as a response or countermeasures to China's assertiveness and expansionism in the Indo-Pacific. In the meanwhile, the 'ASEAN Centrality' would be questionable with the emergence of various groupings.

In the middle of diverse strategies or visions on the Indo-Pacific, India and ASEAN have their own ones, respectively India's Indo-Pacific Oceans Initiative (IPOI) and the ASEAN Outlook on Indo-Pacific (AOIP). Actually, the IPOI and the AOIP share similarities in approach and have the potential to complement and enhance each other. In a working paper drafted by a group of leading Indian experts, they compared and pointed out the key elements of the IPOI and the AOIP and suggested various fields of cooperation where India and ASEAN/Viet Nam could work together, including (i) Maritime cooperation, (ii) Connecting (connecting the connectivities), (iii) the United Nations Sustainable Development Goals 2030 and (iv) Economic and other areas of cooperation (Chauhan *et al.*, 2020).

Trend of Minilateralism and Role of the QUAD

Arguably, the QUAD (an informal strategic forum comprising of the United States, Japan, India and Australia) may be formalised or institutionalised, to some extent, raising concern on the role of ASEAN-led mechanisms. However, there is still room for further collaboration. Indeed, recently, the QUAD leaders announced a series of collective commitments which could be welcomed by the Southeast Asia countries. For instance, the Indo-Pacific Partnership for Maritime Domain Awareness (IPMDA) was a major maritime initiative, offering a "near-real-time, integrated, and cost-effective maritime domain awareness picture," integrating three critical regions in the Indo-Pacific (the Pacific Islands, Southeast Asia and the Indian Ocean region) (White House, Fact Sheet: Quad Leaders' Tokyo Summit 2022). Although it has not got the roadmap for implementation yet, the IPMDA, at least, indicated the QUAD's commitment to counter dark fleets' activities and could serve as an effective tool to promote maritime transparency. India, with its expertise, technology and experience through the Information Fusion Centre–Indian Ocean Region (IFC-IOR) (Do, 2023), could help Southeast Asian countries, including Viet Nam at the bilateral level or through connecting with the QUAD in the field of MDA cooperation.

Another potential avenue for strengthening maritime security cooperation between the QUAD and ASEAN member states may lie in collaborating on the development of undersea cable systems in the Indo-Pacific region. At the 2023 QUAD Leaders' Summit, the QUAD partnership for cable connectivity and resilience was announced, representing a shared commitment to undersea cables as a priority for regional infrastructures. In fact, ensuring submarine cables' security attracts the attention and interest of many countries because of its pivotal role in maritime and digital connectivity. Therefore, in the coming years, India, as a QUAD member, could foster further collaboration between the QUAD and ASEAN in the field of MDA or submarine cable security when these QUAD initiatives are solidly established (Hemrajani, 2023).

Conclusion

The paper has highlighted the long-term relationship between Viet Nam and India after more than 50 years of establishing diplomatic ties. Both countries demonstrated their strategic trust and political will through high-level statements and visions. The comprehensive strategic partnership covers all areas; among them, the defence and security cooperation is the first pillar and the maritime cooperation is a key component. The paper has analysed this partnership within a broader strategic context, characterised by a number of strategic dynamics, intertwined with various perspectives on the Indo-Pacific region. In light of the various geopolitical tensions and flashpoints around the world, such as the Taiwan Strait, the Red Sea/Hormuz Strait, and the Russia-Ukraine conflict, it is important to uphold the rule of law, to ensure unimpeded supply chains and to preserve peace, stability and prosperity. Viet Nam and India should, on one hand, keep moving on this right track on the bilateral level; on the other hand, they could enhance their relationship through various regional platforms in which they participate, reaffirming and supporting the 'ASEAN Centrality.'

References

Australian Government, Infrastructure: https://www.pmc.gov.au/resources/quad-leaders-summit-2023/infrastructure.

Bora, Aman, *Growing India-Viet Nam Defence Relations: A Concern for China*. 22/8/2023: https://orcasia.org/article/401/growing-india-vietnam-defence-relations

Daily Pionner, *Chinese Trawlers Jeopardise India's Maritime Security*. 2021, https://channel16.dryadglobal.com/chinese-trawlers-jeopardise-indias-maritime-security

Do, Hoang, *How to Help ASEAN Address South China Sea 'Gray-zone' Challenges*, 25/9/2023, https://www.usip.org/publications/2023/09/how-help-asean-address-south-china-sea-gray-zone-challenges

Ebbighausen, Rodion, *China Provokes India with a New Official Map*, 30/8/2023, https://www.dw.com/en/china-provokes-india-with-a-new-official-map/a-52620520

Embassy of India in Ha Noi, *Visit of Indian Naval Ships to Da Nang Port, Vietnam*, 19/5/2023: https://www.indembassyhanoi.gov.in/news_letter_detail/?id=210

Embassy of India in Hanoi, *Inauguration of Army Software Park in Nha Trang*, 2021: https://www.indembassyhanoi.gov.in/event_detail/?eventid=414#:~:text=The%20new%20building%20of%20the,presence%20of%20Ambassador%20Pranay%20Verma.

Full Joint Statement between Viet Nam-India in 2018, https://en.baochinhphu.vn/full-joint-statement-between-vn-india-11133760.htm

Funaiole, Matthew; Hart, Brian and Powers-Riggs, Aidan, *Surveying the Seas: China's Dual-Use Research Operations in the Indian Ocean*, 10/1/2024: https://features.csis.org/hiddenreach/china-indian-ocean-research-vessels/

Hemrajani, Asha, *The QUAD Partnership for Cable Connectivity and Resilience*, RSIS, 17/11/2023: https://www.rsis.edu.sg/rsis-publication/cens/the-quad-partnership-for-cable-connectivity-and-resilience/.

India-Viet Nam Joint Vision for Peace, Prosperity and People in 2020, https://www.indembassyhanoi.gov.in/news_letter_detail/?id=150

Joint Statement Philipines-India, 29/6/2023: https://www.mea.gov.in/bilateral-documents.htm?dtl/36743/Joint_Statement_on_the_5th_IndiaPhilippines_Joint_Commission_on_Bilateral_Cooperation

Khanh Nguyen, *3rd India-Viet Nam Maritime Security Dialogue*, VTV. 31/5/2023: https://english.vtv.vn/news/3rd-india-vietnam-maritime-security-dialogue-20230601235542961.htm

Luke, Ashok Alex, *India's Concern over China's growing assertiveness in the Indo-Pacific*, https://www.ipcircle.org/op-eds/india%E2%80%99s-concern-over-china%E2%80%99s-growing-assertiveness-in-the-indo-pacific-.

MEA India, Statement on Award of Arbitral Tribunal on South China Sea, 12/7/2016: https://www.mea.gov.in/press-releases.htm?dtl/27019/statement+on+award+of+arbitral+tribunal+on+south+china+sea+under+annexure+vii+of+unclos

Miglani, Sanjeev and Torode, Greg, *India to build satellite tracking station in Viet Nam that offers eye on China*, 2016: https://www.reuters.com/article/idUSKCN0V30B3/#:~:text=NEW%20DELHI%2FHONG%20KONG%20(Reuters,China%20Sea%2C%20Indian%20officials%20said.

Minh Vu, *Navies of Viet Nam and India Conduct Joint Exercises*, 19/8/2021: https://hanoitimes.vn/navies-of-vietnam-and-india-conduct-joint-exercises-318416.html

Pant, Harsh V., *Locating the Mutual Logistics Support Agreement in India-Australia Strategic Relations*, ORF, 2019. https://www.orfonline.org/research/locating-the-mutual-logistics-support-agreement-in-india-australia-strategic-relations

Peri, Dinakar, *India and Viet Nam sign mutual logistics agreement*, 2022: https://www.thehindu.com/news/national/india-vietnam-ink-military-logistics-support-pact-vision-document-to-expand-defence-ties/article65506502.ece

Peri, Dinakar, *India gifts missile corvette INS Kirpan to Vietnam*, The Hindu, 19/6/2023: https://www.thehindu.com/news/national/india-gifts-missile-corvette-ins-kirpan-to-vietnam/article66986653.ece#

Pradeep, Chauhan; De, Prabir; Parmar, Sarabjeet Singh; Kumarasamy, Durairaj; *Indo-Pacific Cooperation: AOIP and IPOI*, AIC and RIS, 2020: https://aseanindiacentre.org.in/sites/default/files/Publication/AIC%20Working%20Paper%20October%20 2020_0.pdf

Sakhuja, Vijay, *China Expands its Maritime Footprint in the Indian Ocean through its Fishing Fleet*, 2021: https://www.defstrat.com/magazine_articles/china-expands-its-maritime-footprint-in-the-indian-ocean-through-its-fishing-fleet/

Sharma, Rakesh, *China: Coercion as National Policy*, 31/1/2022: https://www.vifindia.org/article/2022/january/31/china-coercion-as-national-policy

Singh, Rahul, *India hands over fully operational warship to Vietnam*, 23/7/2023: https://www.hindustantimes.com/india-news/indian-navy-decommissions-ins-kirpan-and-gifts-it-to-vietnam-to-deepen-defence-ties-and-counter-chinese-expansion-101690088942895.html

The Economic Times, *India to skip China's Belt and Road Forum for a Third Time*, 16/10/2023: https://economictimes.indiatimes.com/news/economy/foreign-trade/india-to-skip-chinas-belt-and-road-forum-for-a-third-time/articleshow/104466383.cms?from=mdr

VNA, *Viet Nam Coast Guard vessel pays first visit to India*, 2018: https://en.vietnamplus.vn/vietnam-coast-guard-vessel-pays-first-visit-to-india/139357.vnp.

VOV, "Ấn Độ chuẩn bị bàn giao tàu hải quân cho Việt Nam," 9/7/2023: https://vov.vn/the-gioi/an-do-chuan-bi-ban-giao-tau-hai-quan-cho-viet-nam-post1031560.vov.

White House, *Fact Sheet: Quad Leaders' Tokyo Summit 2022*, https://www.whitehouse.gov/briefing-room/statements-releases/2022/05/23/fact-sheet-quad-leaders-tokyo-summit-2022/

About the Contributors

Dr Dharish David, Associate Faculty, SIM-Global Education, Singapore
Dharish David is an associate faculty for the University of London at the Singapore Institute of Management – Global Education (SIM-GE), teaching courses relating to political economy. In his recent role, he was the industry research manager for a Japanese startup in Singapore, handling an analyst team covering India, ASEAN, and China across 16 main industry verticals. He previously worked at the Asian Development Bank Institute in Tokyo as a research associate working on Green Growth and Infrastructure Development in Asia. He received his doctorate from Waseda University (Tokyo, Japan) specialising in infrastructure development and financing. He has written widely on Asian political economy, economic development, infrastructure development, sustainable development, and international relations. He has also consulted for projects on technology policy, sustainable development, and economic research for regional think tanks and research firms. He has written several book chapters, academic articles, business insight, and thematic reports, apart from regularly writing short insight pieces and op-eds in renowned platforms such as SCMP, East Asia Forum, and Global Policy.

Mr Abhisek Kumar Pandey, Student, University of London, SIM-Global Education, Singapore
Abhishek Kumar Pandey is a graduate of the University of London in Accounting and Finance. He is a Digital Products and Transformation

intern with PwC (India), and is primarily involved there in strategic and business research. Besides finance and emerging technologies, he has a deep interest in international relations and trade.

Rear Admiral (Retd) Jude Ong, Professor of Praxis, Ateneo School of Government, Ateneo de Manila University, the Philippines

RAdm Rommel Jude Ong (Retd) is currently affiliated with the Ateneo School of Government (ASOG) as a Professor of Praxis in the Academic Department and a Senior Research Fellow with the Ateneo Policy Centre. He was co-lead investigator in research on Chinese political warfare and in a two-phase study entitled: Toward Increased and Stable Investments in National Security in the Philippines: An Analysis of Trends, Allocations, and Policy Options in Philippine Defense Spending. He was also the lead researcher on a study in ASEAN mini-laterals for the University of the Philippines Centre for Integrative Development Studies (UPCIDS). He edited a book entitled "Security Sector Reform and Governance in the Philippines," which was written as a project of the National Defense College of the Philippines. Recently, he contributed a chapter in the book Martial Law in the Philippines: Lessons and Legacies 1972-2022. His last posting was as Vice Commander of the Philippine Navy until his compulsory retirement. He has successfully commanded three (3) commissioned naval vessels, and later the Naval Intelligence Security Force, the Naval Task Forces 11 and 80, the Director of the Fleet Marine Warfare Centre, and the Naval Forces West, which has operational jurisdiction over the West Philippine Sea. He has also occupied senior staff positions such as the Assistant Chief of Staff for Naval Operations (N3), the Assistant Deputy Chief for Joint Operations (AJ3) and the Naval Inspector General. RADM Ong is a graduate of the Philippine Military Class of 1987. He completed his advanced training at the US Naval War College and his Senior Executive Course on National Security (MNSA-equivalent) at the National Defence College of the Philippines. He completed his Masters in Development Management at the Asian Institute of Management.

Ms Nguyen Hoang Anh Thu, PhD Student, Lee Kuan Yew School of Public Policy, National University of Singapore (NUS)

Nguyen Hoang Anh Thu is pursuing a PhD in Public Policy at the National University of Singapore. Concurrently, she is a 2024 Blue Security Fellow at La Trobe University and a member of the Young Leaders Program at the Pacific Forum. She holds an MA in Transnational Governance from the European University Institute and a BA in International Relations from Tokyo International University. Previously, she was an intern at the Fisheries and Aquaculture Unit, Organisation for Economic Co-operation and Development (OECD). Her research interests include International Relations of the Asia-Pacific, maritime security, and public policy.

Ms Jeslyn Tan, Researcher, Centre of Maritime Security and Diplomacy, Maritime Institute of Malaysia (MIMA)

Jeslyn Tan is a Researcher at the Centre of Maritime Security and Diplomacy at the Maritime Institute of Malaysia (MIMA). Her main research interests include ASEAN-major power relations, Indo-Pacific geopolitics, regional multilateralism, and maritime security in Southeast Asia. She is also a participant in the Indo-Pacific Maritime GENIE (Governance Expanded Network for Innovation and Education) Program funded by the Australian Government and a Young Leader of the Pacific Forum. Furthermore, she was a Security Research Fellow in the EU-funded EU-ASEAN Think Tank Dialogue (EANGAGE) Project. Previously, she received a Master of Arts in International Relations from the University of Warwick, UK.

Dr Nguyen Thi Lan Huong, Assistant Director General; Director, Centre for International Law East Sea (South China Sea) Institute, Diplomatic Academy of Viet Nam (DAV)

Nguyen Thi Lan Huong is a Senior Research Fellow and Director of the Centre for International Law of the East Sea Institute, Diplomatic Academy of Viet Nam. She was deputy director of the Centre for International Cooperation of the same institute (January 2020–May 2022). She got her LLM in International and European Law in

2011 from the University of Nice-Sophia Antipolis (France) and a PhD degree in International Law from the Diplomatic Academy of Viet Nam. Her research field is Public International Law, Law of the Sea and the South China Sea issue.

Commodore R. S. Vasan IN (Retd), Director General, Chennai Centre for China Studies (C3S) & Regional Director, National Maritime Foundation, Tamil Nadu (NMF-TN)

An Alumnus of the Defence Services Staff College, the Naval War College and the International Visitor Leadership Programme, Commodore Seshadri Vasan has a distinguished service of over 34 years in the Navy and the Coast Guard. His appointments include command of warships, two major air stations and a maritime air squadron. He has participated both in the 1971 war and IPKF operations. He was an instructor at the Naval War College, India. Prior to retirement, he was the Regional Commander of the Indian Coast Guard Region East overseeing EEZ Patrol, SAR, Anti- Piracy, Fisheries protection, Maritime Border Control, Marine Pollution prevention and other maritime tasks in the Bay of Bengal. Post retirement he has served in many think tanks and is a regular speaker at many International and national conferences. He was also the Chairman of the Aeronautical Society of India, Chennai Charter and the Director of the Asian Bureau of the World Border Police, Director of TEXCO and President of the Navy Foundation Chennai Chapter. He has many publications to his credit in journals, websites, edited books and media. The details of the papers are at https://centerforasiastudies.academia.edu/SeshadriVasan. The think tanks that he has served in include the Observer Research Foundation where he steered the Maritime Security Programme (presently redesignated as the Maritime Policy Initiative) and the Centre for Asia Studies where he was the Head of Strategy and Security Studies. He is presently the Director General of the Chennai Centre of China Studies and the Regional Director of the National Maritime Foundation Tamil Nadu. He has been a visiting faculty at the Indian Maritime University, Academy of Maritime Education and Training, Great Lakes Institute of Management and Hindustan Institute of Engineering Technology. He is on the Board of Advisors at the Madras University, the Stella Maris College and the Puducherry University.

Dr N. Manoharan Professor and Director, Centre for East Asian Studies (CEAS), Christ (Deemed to be) University, Bengaluru

Dr N. Manoharan is a Professor and Director at the Centre for East Asian Studies (CEAS), Christ (Deemed to be) University, Bengaluru. He earlier served at the National Security Council Secretariat (NSCS), PMO and Ministry of Defence, Government of India. He was a South Asia Fellow at the East-West Centre, Washington and is a recipient of the Mahbub-ul Haq International Award for research. His areas of interest include internal security, terrorism, Sri Lanka, Maldives, human rights, ethnic conflicts, multiculturalism, security sector reforms, the Indo-Pacific and conflict resolution. His main books include: Developing Democracies; Counterterror Laws and Security: Lessons from India and Sri Lanka; Security Deficit: A Comprehensive Internal Security Strategy for India; India's War on Terror; SAARC: Towards Greater Connectivity; Ethnic Violence and Human Rights in Sri Lanka; and Counterterrorism Legislation in Sri Lanka: Evaluating Efficacy. His forthcoming book is the 'Federal Aspects of Foreign Policy: The Role of Tamil Nadu Fishermen Issue in India-Sri Lanka Relations' (Routledge). He writes regularly for leading newspapers, websites and reputed peer-reviewed international journals.

Ms Sruthi Sadhasivam, Research Officer, Chennai Centre for China Studies (C3S) & Coordinator of the C3S-CEAS ASEAN Conference

Sruthi Sadhasivam is a researcher at the Chennai Centre for China Studies (C3S). She graduated with an MA in International Studies from Christ (Deemed to be) University, Bengaluru. Her major areas of research pertain to non-traditional security threats including climate change, and issues concerning maritime security, border security and human security. She has published her work in the National Institute of Advanced Studies (NIAS) and Chennai Centre for China Studies (C3S). As part of the Young-IPRI Workshop, she has presented a paper titled 'Conflict in Central Sahel: Reasons for Protraction of Conflict' at Pondicherry University. Recently, she participated in a Roundtable Dialogue on 'Reimagining the Indo-Pacific Using an Inclusive Lens' where she discussed the role played by China in the Indo-Pacific and the blurring lines between traditional & non-traditional security threats in the Indo-Pacific Region (IOR). Her paper on India's climate leadership in the Indo-Pacific Region has been published in the Journal of the Indian Ocean Region (JIOR), a Scopus-indexed journal. She has co-authored a book chapter on Post-Truth Politics for the book titled 'Encyclopedia of New Populism and Responses in the 21st Century,' a Springer publication. Further, she is deeply passionate about developing conflict trackers and has written on China's grey zone warfare in the Indo-Pacific, Taiwan and Pacific Island states and China's endeavours at the eastern sector of the Sino-Indian Border.

About the Book

The book unravels the Southeast Asian outlook on China's pursuits in the Indo-Pacific Region (IOR). It is organised into two thematic sections: the first addresses the Southeast Asian perspective on China's maritime and economic ambitions, and the second investigates India-ASEAN cooperation in the Indo-Pacific's security ecosystem.

For this purpose, the volume brings together expert contributions from the Philippines, Singapore, Vietnam, and Malaysia, providing a multifaceted analysis of Southeast Asia's China dilemma from economic, defense, and security vantage points.

With ASEAN becoming a pertinent investment destination, it becomes significant to study the broader implications of ASEAN states bilateral and multilateral trade dynamics. To achieve this objective, the book uses a data-driven analysis to uncover the latest developments and patterns in ASEAN trade. Further, in the era of hybrid warfare with the South China Sea becoming a recurring hotspot and Philippines the most threatened, the book addresses various issues concerning China's maritime militia, submarine patrols, food and economic security of ASEAN states by studying affected States' challenges and policy responses. Further, with Southeast Asia being India's extended neighbourhood, the volume illuminates the evolving India-ASEAN relationship, focusing on shared interests and emerging complexities.

By and large, this book serves as a crucial reference for policy makers, scholars and students seeking to comprehend Southeast Asian perspectives on China's IOR engagements and evolving Indo-ASEAN relations.